ARIZONA

off the beaten path!

Stories and Photos by

Thelma Heatwole

author of

Ghost Towns & Historical Haunts in Arizona

Golden West Publishers

FRONT COVER . . . Court House Rock on Eagle Tail Mountain approach

BACK COVER . . . Box Canyon, northeast of Florence, Az.

Front and back cover artwork by Bruce Robert Fischer

Physical hazards may be encountered in visiting areas of ARIZONA-OFF THE
BEATEN PATH, particularly old mining localities. Land ownerships and road
conditions change over the years. Readers should take proper precautions and
make local inquiries, as author and publishers cannot accept responsibility for
such matters.

Library of Congress Cataloging in Publication Data

Heatwole, Thelma
   Arizona--off the beaten path!

   Includes index.
   1. Arizona--Description and travel--1951-1980--
Addresses, essays, lectures. 2. Arizona--Description
and travel--1981-   --Addresses, essays, lectures.
3. Arizona--Social life and customs--Addresses, essays,
lectures. 4. Country life--Arizona--Addresses, essays,
lectures. 5. Heatwole, Thelma, 1912-   --Addresses,
essays, lectures. I. Title.
F815.H4 1982   979.1'05   82-11772
ISBN 0-914846-13-2

Printed in the United States of America

Golden West Publishers
4113 N. Longview Ave.
Phoenix, AZ. 85014, USA

This book is dedicated to our good friends
John and Winifred Lynch
who accompanied us on many backwoods trips
and share our enjoyment of fabulous Arizona.

John and Winifred Lynch (at left) are pictured
with author Thelma Heatwole and her husband, Don.

PRECAUTIONS

- "Backwoods" visitors must be cautious.
- Some areas are pocked with *mines, potholes, old wells.* Don't forget *the desert washes that can flood* and the *quicksand* that may lurk in riverbeds, streams and water holes.
- Gas, food, water and first aid supplies must be sufficient for the length of your trip, and longer.
- Keep an eye out for *snakes* and other denizens of the remote country.

Salty beach along remote area of Salt River

CONTENTS

Punch and Judy rocks

INTRODUCTION

Arizona offers a unique package for travelers and explorers without racking up too many expensive miles in the process. Scenic beauty and outdoor fun combine in fascinating locales.

U.S. Senator Barry Goldwater, speaking at the Heard Museum, phrased it exactly.

"I don't care how long you live in this state, you never get tired of it. And, you never really see it all," he said. "If you have a car, get out and see this state."

Besides Arizona's major scenic attractions—the **Grand Canyon, Sedona's Red Rock Country,** Indian reservations, **Arizona Strip Country**—there are intriguing off-the-beaten path places. This book addresses those scenes.

During my years as an *Arizona Republic* staff reporter with a beat of eight Valley cities, I devoted many weekends and holidays to visiting ghost towns, backwoods scenic places and the headliner attractions. It became a self-imposed quest to combine travel into remote areas with writing about them. Pure adventure was the bonus.

Usually, we traveled with another couple never knowing exactly what would happen along the way. In fact, the unusual, the unexpected added zest to the occasion.

The **Wonderland of Rocks** is a case in point. We arrived at this scenic marvel on an early December morning. It was brisk and so cold —a time many sensible people preferred the warmth of their own hearth. The shocker came when we learned we faced an eight-mile one-way hike. After a huddle, the four of us agreed we were able and anxious to make the hike.

We drove to **Massai Point** at 6,720 feet, left the car and began the descent, traipsing at times through patches of snow. About half way through the monument we reached the trail that led to the "Heart of the Rocks," where the famed "Punch and Judy" and other fantastic formations abound. We were awestruck! At times, our huffing was so great we stopped to allow our breathing to stabilize.

Finally, we walked into the ranger station. We were told that only 15 percent of visitors walk through the monument. After retrieving our car with the help of the ranger, we broiled steaks over a grill in the picnic area. By that time, darkness had closed in and my knit shirt, sweat shirt and windbreaker coat combined to combat the cold.

That evening our legs were so sore and stiff we could scarcely walk normally. We were not the least alarmed. The next day we were at it again, making a mile-and-a-half hike to reach old **Fort Bowie.**

* * * * *

Then, there was the time we traveled for a profile look at the community of **Arivaca** in Southern Arizona. All morning, townspeople had observed strangers motoring through town bound for a hippie wedding along the **California Gulch.** We decided to join the procession.

The trail off the main road was so rough that many before us had left their cars, boarding sturdier transportation to the backwoods wedding scene. By the time our Jeep arrived, the ceremony was over.

It was a strange procession of guests coming down the hill. One youth was in bib overalls and without a shirt, and a pretty girl clutching a bouquet was the bridesmaid. The radiant bridal pair talked readily with us. The bride wore an ankle-length gown of fine white material and brown sandals. The groom carried a guitar and his bride's white slippers.

The sizable wedding party, after dining on chicken, macaroni salad and vodka, left finally in a whirl of dust and barking dogs. We departed somewhat mesmerized, contemplating a segment of society that was part of the American scene.

* * * * *

Probably the most hazardous trip was the "Way to the Ovens." The episode started out as a lark. Later, our four-wheel drive vehicle was embroiled in a tough assignment. The road became scarcely discernible and beset with rocks, dips, chuckholes. At times we built up the road with rocks.

Don, my husband, maneuvered the worst roads of our "backwoods" adventure careers. Sometimes it seemed we would not reach our objective.

Once, the driver lost his cool and suggested that the two chattering women passengers walk ahead—far ahead. Seriously, he said he would never attempt the trip again unless it were a case of "life and death."

When we arrived at the spectacular giant ovens, a stone's throw from the **Gila River,** our companion broiled steaks to perfection. We could scarcely enjoy them. We were aware we could not retrace our travel before dark. There seemed no way of crossing the river.

Wondering if home folks would start missing us, we heard motors approaching from the direction of the river. In the end, the helpful jeepsters guided us to a shallow crossing of the river. The day was saved. (On a second trip—in 1981—the **Gila** was deep and swift, utterly impassable.)

* * * * *

Once, in another difficult terrain maneuver, I bailed out from the vehicle to capture the unexpected photo shot—should there be one. Don, anxious about the driving, was heard to mutter, "If I rolled this Jeep down the hill, she'd probably keep right on taking pictures." I probably would. Such are the lengths a camera buff reaches.

Really, though, such fun banter helped us keep our cool in times of tempest.

* * * * *

Of course, we ruptured our gas tank twice before finally undergirding it with a substantial steel plate. Fortunately, our Jeep is equipped with two 20-gallon tanks. Only once did we run out of gas.

* * * * *

Sometimes we encounter novelty—like the time on the **Coronado Trail** near **Sheep Saddle,** where two fawns grazed in the forest a short distance from the roadway. We inched the car to a quiet stop, the fawns watching us quizzically. Trying to be calm, I switched from wide angle to telephoto lens. By that time the fawns were satisfied we were harmless. They turned their backsides toward us and continued their feeding. We honked the horn gently and the creatures took a brief look at us. In the excitement, however, I moved the camera and the photo was out of focus. However, it still serves as a souvenir of a gentle moment.

* * * * *

Our trip to **Woodruff** was targeted at seeing the petrified wood fence at the Earl Crofford home. Never have we been accorded such hospitality. The Croffords treated us to a sumptuous feast—roast beef, fresh garden peas, beets, potatoes, homemade rolls and blueberry cobbler. Their cellar abounded in canned grape jelly, cocktail onions, pickled okra, tomatoes, their own dried beans and red chili peppers—to name a few gourmet items.

Afterwards we toured **Blue Butte,** areas of the **Silver Creek** and the **Little Colorado** and saw astounding pictographs that relatively few Arizonans have seen.

* * * * *

Stories in this book are as they appeared in the *Arizona Republic*, with little revision.

In these days when most people are concerned about conserving gas and its high price tag, it is time to focus interest on the Arizona scene. No place surpasses its natural wonders.

This book details the fun of capturing them.

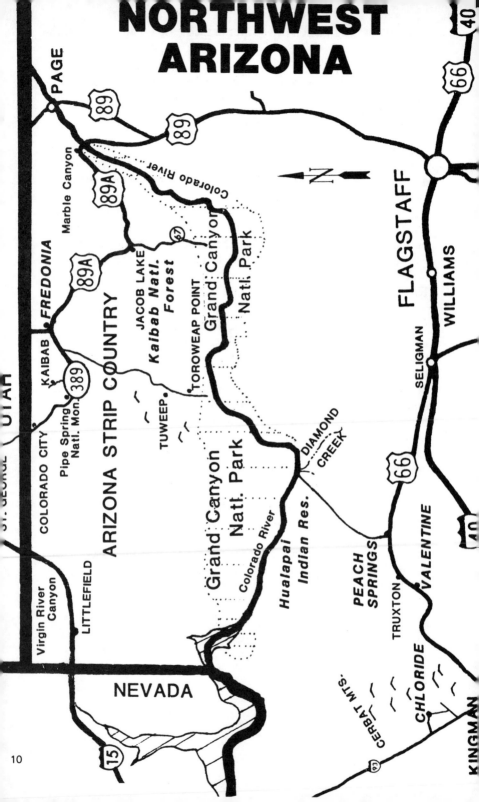

NORTHWEST ARIZONA

CHLORIDE
old mines and new!

This old mining town, four miles east of **Grasshopper** and **U.S. Highway 93** Junction, is backgrounded by the **Cerbat Mountains.** And, right on Tennessee Avenue on **Chloride's** main street, cottontails dash in front of cars.

Coveys of quail parade across the roads. Once a mother quail was leading a line of babies so tiny they could scarcely hurry.

At the corner of Second and Tennessee, a flag stands atop the **Chloride** Post Office, altitude, 4,009 ft. Adjoining is the Russell's Chloride General Store with an inviting front porch bench.

On another corner was a tiny building, looking much like an outhouse, with a sign that said "Ye Old Chloride Town House."

The historic town, with some 250 people, has a claim to fame that sets the place apart from the usual mining towns—even those of 1860 vintage.

It's the Roy Purcell murals on rock cliffs in the **Cerbats,** about two miles from town. In fact, **Chloride** has become known as the home of the paintings. A dirt road corkscrews through the buckbrush and holly-clad hills to the striking surrealistic works on the cliffs. The panorama is in vivid orange, blue, red and yellow.

Artist Purcell began the art in 1966. An inscription sets the tone for the work: "Images from an inward search for self." The artistry is well worth the visit. And, in an interesting contrast at the scene, there

Along Chloride's main street

Rocky cliffs reveal artwork of Roy Purcell.

are ancient Indian pictographs.

Chloride resident Cyrus Patterson, a former miner at the old Tennessee Mine, served as patron of the arts by providing paints for the Purcell murals.

Glenna Auld Alger, realtor and bar operator, lived here as a child.

"My dad and brother took the Tennessee down the last 200 feet in 1948. That was the last dying gasp of the Tennessee," she said.

The **Tennessee Mine,** some 1600 ft. deep, is now almost filled with water. It is owned by the El Paso Gas Company, Mrs. Alger said.

The **Duval Mine,** an open pit operation about seven miles away and owned by Pennzoil, is active. **Chloride,** at one time, was a distribution point for several mines in the vicinity.

Arizona Place Names notes that **Chloride** was named for the type silver ore found in the area. In 1864, **Chloride** was a mining camp, but as additional mines developed, it became a town and by 1900 had a population of more than 2,000.

Patterson, who worked at the Tennessee 37 years, said that **Chloride** is a quiet place.

"That's the reason I like it. I don't think I could take it in the city. And, we have some fine people here," he added.

Will you be my
VALENTINE, AZ?

Many Arizona residents are surprised to learn there is a community in the state called **Valentine** (zip code 86437).

While relatively few Arizonans know about **Valentine,** which is located beside U.S. **66** between **Kingman** and **Peach Springs** in the northwest part of the state, people back east do. They send valentines galore to be mailed from the small post office.

The postmaster one year started out to count the Valentines that came in. She gave up. They ran into the thousands. Postal-wise, the traffic is almost as heavy as at Christmas. The office in 1973 served about 100 patrons.

In 1970, a romantic young couple from Washington arrived in the tiny hamlet on a mission of the heart.

They were married on Valentine's Day in **Valentine** and in the "Valentine State" (so called because Arizona was admitted to the union on Valentine's Day in 1912).

The couple made advance arrangements and a judge performed the ceremony at the home of a missionary at the Indian Agency here. Afterward, their wedding announcements were postmarked and mailed with the Valentine postal cancellation.

A stamp club from Pennsylvania sent a batch of valentines to be cancelled "Valentine" and returned in a package for later distribution. Other persons sent affectionate greetings and asked that their valentines be mailed Feb. 10 or 12 or on Valentine's Day.

The post office was a part of a trading post. The store faded away, but not the postal service.

Two little bells tinkle over the doorway when patrons arrive. Many stop to chat and most show up every weekday. Sometimes the Continental and Greyhound busses stop. Mail is trucked in from **Kingman.**

Valentine has nothing to do with the day set aside for lovers. The place was named for Robert G. Valentine, commissioner of Indian Affairs from 1908 to 1910.

According to *Arizona Place Names,* a post office was established at **Truxton** (at the Truxton Canyon Subagency) in 1901. The name was changed (and the location) to **Valentine** on Feb. 24, 1910.

On May 14, 1900, some 660 acres of land were set aside and an Indian school was built on the land. The brick building no longer serves as a school, but the agency is headquarters for four Indian tribes in northwestern Arizona.

14 VALENTINE (Northwest Arizona)

DIAMOND CREEK
in the rough

Diamond Creek merges with the **Colorado River** on a novel chunk of Arizona's scenery and history.

It is located on the **Hualapai Indian Reservation** not far below **Grand Canyon National Park** where there used to be a popular hotel and beach.

The area is remote and reached by a 20-mile trail out of **Peach Springs,** which is located on **U.S. 66** in Mohave County, northwestern Arizona. Creek beds are criss-crossed enroute.

Monroe Beecher, director of wildlife and recreation for the Hualapai Tribe, and Mrs. Beecher, chatted with us at the agency office in **Peach Springs.** It is there that travelers obtain a permit for sightseeing and fishing. Arizona fishing licenses also are required.

The trip should be made before the weather gets too warm but not in bad weather or rain. Four-wheel drive vehicles are recommended.

Mrs. Beecher also advised persons wanting to make the trip to contact the agency before driving to **Peach Springs.** Roads to the

In the distance looms Diamond Creek 15

Crossing Diamond Creek

beach sometimes are washed out.

The road from **Peach Springs** drops from 4,800 feet, passing colorful cliffs with a Grand Canyon-look.

Vegetation changed with descent from pinon and juniper to prickly pear and barrel cacti, mesquite, cat claw and a sprinkling of yellow flowers.

Mrs. Mary Nelson of nearby **Truxton,** who in her childhood lived at the **Gold Road** mining camp, once told me that after her marriage she lived in **Peach Springs** and her husband drove a stage to the hotel by **Diamond Creek.**

Diamond Point Mountain, a landmark peak, loomed miles ahead.

Beecher reported that fishermen angle for catfish and trout. A project was under planning to establish a departure point on the **Colorado River** for rubber raft trips to the **Lake Mead** area.

Near the junction of the creek and the **Colorado** there were two flood-eroded ramadas and visitors in a truck and jeep.

At Diamond Point along the Colorado River

SPECTACULAR HIGHWAY
and its gorgeous gorge
(near Littlefield)

Arizona's most spectacular highway must be the 21.5 mile stretch of Interstate 15 through the extreme northwest corner of the state to St. George, Utah.

But, since the **Grand Canyon** separates the highway from all Arizona metropolitan areas, Arizonans wishing to see the gorge, through which the highway threads, and its sheer canyon walls, must drive to Nevada or Utah.

A three-mile stretch of the highway through the rugged **Virgin River Canyon** cost $100 an inch and, in 1973, it was said to be the most expensive highway construction job, excluding tunnels, in the 41,000-mile national interstate system.

The highway cuts through massive mountains to expose sheer walls of varied rock strata. Each curve offers new vistas in pinks, beige and purples.

The river cuts a deep, sinuous canyon through the spine of the **Virgin Mountains.** In places the canyon rim towers 750 feet above the canyon bottom which is no more than 70 feet wide. Cuts as high as 350 feet were excavated in solid limestone.

The new highway is the shortest route between **Littlefield** and St. George, chopping the distance from 40 to 26.6 miles.

Highway officials said final cost estimates for the 21.5 stretch will range from $50 million to $65 million.

The highway through the gorge was under study for years, but it was not until 1959 that the Arizona Highway Department retained consultants to make detailed study and field survey of the route.

Arizona originally opposed putting the road through the canyon because it could have been built just below the north rim through **Cedar Pockets** at less cost and with an increased length of only three miles. But the U.S. Bureau of Public Roads, now known as the Federal Highway Association, insisted on the canyon route.

Arizona officials were not pleased that the route skirts **Littlefield,** the only Arizona community it could serve. **Littlefield** residents still (in 1973) seek a second exchange on the east side of the river before the highway enters the gorge area.

The interstate system, according to Robert Hedlund of the Arizona Highway Department, is financed on a 95 to 5 basis by the federal government. **Interstate 15** is an important link between Los Angeles, Las Vegas and Salt Lake City.

Littlefield School plays community role

Arizona's participation in the final phase came through a loan of federal money from Utah and has been paid back from its federal allocations.

The job had many hazards. Hedlund recounted one incident that occurred while building the bridge across the **Virgin River** at **Littlefield.** Workmen were driving a 40-foot bridge pile and had another 10 feet to go when they quit for the night. When they returned, the pile was swallowed by quicksand.

Two **Littlefield** residents expressed concern that the new highway would be dangerous because of the impact of high winds in the gorge and falling rocks. Hedlund said highway engineers had made an extensive study of rock fallings in the area. "This has not been ignored by engineers in planning the road," he said.

The Arizona portion of the highway will provide rest areas at Cedar Pocket in coordination with a Bureau of Land Management project for campground development. The project is Arizona's first joint-use recreation facility.

Divider separates lanes of $100-an-inch freeway through Virgin River Canyon   19

TOROWEAP POINT
the long road to Short Creek

Toroweap, a point overlooking the Colorado River 3,000 feet below, is a majestic sight and well-calculated to keep viewers on guard.

It is reached by a jolting dusty road in a remote section of the **Arizona Strip Country.**

The strip country, separated from the rest of Arizona by the Colorado River, has been called one of the loneliest places in America. But its very isolation is an attraction.

The vast wilderness, south of the Utah border and roughly between **Marble Canyon** and **Colorado City,** boasts forests, vermillion cliffs, bizarre mountain formations, empty valleys and spectacular scenery.

The **Tuweep** district, in Grand Canyon National Park, is reached through Bureau of Land Management (BLM) country. The **Toroweap** overlook, 6.5 racking miles from the ranger station in **Tuweep,** was the target of an adventure-seeking party.

The road through a section of the **Strip Country** opens off **Highway 389** between **Fredonia** and **Pipe Springs,** with **Toroweap Point** some 56 miles off the main highway.

Turning off the highway with a fresh start in the early morning out of **Fredonia,** the travelers noted the beauty of the lonely country, its mountains backgrounding stretches of rippled plateaus.

The unimproved road contained narrow bridges, washes and even mud holes. At times the road to **Tuweep** and on **Mount Trumbull** was too narrow for another car to pass.

One surprise was the airstrip before entering the national park. Passengers on the Colorado River are airlifted by helicopter and taken to the airstrip for transportation by small planes. A sign proclaims the isolated terminal as **"Tuweep International Airport."**

John Riffey, the park ranger, lives within sight of the airstrip. He flies a plane to patrol the vast 200,000-acre **Tuweep** district. (Note: Mr. Riffey died since this story was written.)

At **Toroweap,** the rough ride was eclipsed in the awesome sight of the towering cliffs, the famed Colorado River below with **Lava Falls** visible to the west. River craft and helicopter pickups added interest. There were no guard rails, however, which gave spectators a squeamish feeling. It is hardly a place for children.

Riffey said the fact there are no guard rails keeps people from getting "as far out" as they would if there were rails. Riffey did not think visitors would be turned loose if there were a paved road to the place.

Old schoolhouse, once hub of Mt. Trumbull community

"You'd get a clientele that didn't think," he said. "People now are watching. We've never lost anyone yet."

Riffey talked more about the people who come to the area.

"Most people who came in here know what they are doing," he said. "We get a neophyte once in a while who busts a gas tank or oil pan on the road."

Riffey contends that most motorists who brave travel in the area are a "different breed." The ordinary person, he said, would be turned off by the unimproved roads.

A register at the nearby little picnic area (no water available) shows the remote area does attract visitors. There are names from London, Honolulu, Germany, Boston, Connecticut and others.

Riffey said about 2,500 persons a year sign the register.

The strip country contains one of the largest single blocks of BLM land in the west. It is an area that does not get much people pressure.

The expedition should not be tackled without a vehicle in good condition, plenty of gas, water and food. Check first to see which roads are passable. A good idea before going into the area is to get a map of the strip country from the BLM office in Phoenix. Precautions for travel in the remote area are included on the map.

There are many areas, too many for a single day. Our trip included the forest-clad **Mount Trumbull,** a well-known landmark of the west end of the strip and **Nixon Springs.**

The trip was an eye-opener. Acting on advice of one area resident, our party in the four-wheel drive vehicle took a shortcut road out. It almost proved disastrous.

Somehow, along the way, the wrong trail—one that wound over super rough terrain—was chosen. There were anxious moments, and it was the extra tank of gas the vehicle carried that saved the day.

The paved road near **Colorado City** (formerly **Short Creek**) never looked so good.

22   *From Toroweap Point, the Colorado River meanders through canyon wilderness.*

STRIP COUNTRY
loneliest place in America!

Arizona's little known **Strip Country,** in northern recesses of the state, offers changing panorama from **Marble Canyon** and the spectacular **Vermillion Cliffs** to history-steeped **Pipe Springs.**

In between are the pine-scented **Kaibab Forest,** the **North Rim** of the **Grand Canyon,** empty stretches of country and isolated villages. The **Strip** is that part of Arizona north of the **Colorado River.** Within that vast expanse live some 2,000 people. Some claim that the **Strip,** cut off from the rest of Arizona by the **Grand Canyon** and the **Colorado River,** is one of the loneliest places in America.

U.S. 89 above **Flagstaff** runs through the **Navajo Indian Reservation,** a route both desolate and scenic. There are trading posts, lonely hogans, sheep and cattle that are apt to wander on the highway and quaint roadside stands where Indian beads are sold.

U.S. 89 veers to **Page,** and **Strip**-bound travelers head west on **U.S. 89 Alternate.** Beneath **Navajo Bridge,** the **Colorado River** glistens between craggy mountain sides. Beyond, the red cliffs seem laced with purple haze.

Jacob's Lake Inn, elevation 7,925 ft., with motel, dining and curios, is a hub for travelers. **The Lake,** in the heart of the **Kaibab National Forest** on the **Kaibab Plateau,** is an entranceway to the **North Rim** of the **Canyon,** on **Arizona 67** through continuous forest.

Fredonia, with its wide streets and spreading trees, offers small accommodations for travelers. Larger motels and eating places are at Kanab, seven miles from **Fredonia,** in Utah.

Pipe Spring National Monument, 14 miles from **Fredonia** on the **Strip,** was a delight from its cool spring cellar to balcony-fronted rooms around an inner courtyard. The Mormon-built fort there stands amid tall shade trees and spring-fed ponds, a veritable oasis in a land of desert vegetation.

Mormon missionaries to the Indians discovered **Pipe Spring.** Led by Jacob Hamblin, they camped by the spring in the fall of 1858 while enroute to Hopi land.

William "Gunlock Bill" Hamblin shot the bottom out of a smoking pipe to demonstrate his marksmanship, hence the name **Pipe Spring.** Killings by marauding Indians led to abandonment of the spring for a time.

In 1870, President Brigham Young of the Church of Latter-day Saints and his advisors decided to establish a ranch here for raising cattle and production of dairy products for nearby settlements.

Rooms in the museum are furnished with souvenirs from old

Navajo Bridge spans Colorado

spinning wheels to ancient organs and bedsteads. A tap on the telegraph key that sent the first message from the telegraph station in Territorial Arizona on December 15, 1871, brings a replay of that message.

The museum is open from 8 a.m. to 5 p.m. There is no admission charge and there are shaded picnic tables nearby. Lunches should be brought along, as eating accommodations on the **Strip** are few and far between.

There are numerous places to see in the **Strip,** including **Toroweap Point,** where the canyon gorge drops thousands of feet below, and the **Mount Trumbull** area. The only access to these areas is by dirt roads, where, according to reports, some low slung cars could have difficulty.

A ranger said that visitors on unpaved roads should have adequate supplies of gasoline, water and a spare tire. A good rule in traveling through the **Strip,** the U.S. Bureau of Land Management cautioned, is to *inquire locally* and *obtain maps* before venturing on unsurfaced roads.

North of **Pipe Spring** are two small communities—**Kaibab,** an Indian Village, and **Moccasin,** a small Mormon community, with attractive homes and a school house dated 1904.

Colorado City, formerly called **Short Creek,** basks quietly at the end of **Arizona 389** in the **Strip Country.** The well-paved highway passes within a short distance of the community, which straddles the state line.

On a Sunday afternoon, townspeople were resting from their labors. A young boy pedaled through town, a tall milk can perched on the back of his bicycle, and two little girls dressed in Sunday clothes waved to strangers.

Fredonia is 337 miles from **Phoenix.** Travelers should allow a long weekend to visit several points of interest in the **Strip.** Camping facilities are available at **Jacob's Lake.**

Pipe Springs National Monument

Steamboat Rock near Fredonia

N

PRESCOTT

89

ALAMO LAKE

Buckskin Mts.

PARKER

71

WICKENBURG

72

AGUILA

95

WENDEN

60

EAGLE'S EYE

60

QUARTZSITE

WHITE TANK MTNS.

89

95

10

GLENDALE

PALM CANYON

EAGLE TAIL MTNS.

TONOPAH

PHOENIX

95

KOFA NATL. WILDLIFE REFUGE

Painted Rock Historic Park

85

GILA BEND

YUMA

8

SOUTHWEST ARIZONA

85

Republic of Mexico

AJO

WHY

ORGAN PIPE CACTUS

NATL. MON.

85

LUKEVILLE

To Rocky Point

ALAMO LAKE
and a six-pack of burros

Alamo Lake, nestled against the backdrop of the purple-hued **Buckskin Mountains,** glistened and shimmered in the sun.

Hundreds of people were in their campers, trailers, motor homes and tents in the recreation area. They had come to fish, boat, picnic, bask in the sun and relax.

But, for one group of sightseers, the primary goal was to see the wild burros that populate the area.

The sun waned in the west and the zero hour was approaching. A ranger had promised that burros would come out of the hills for their evening drink.

Earlier, Ranger Les Bovee interspersed registering campers with talking about the bothersome animals.

"There's an over population of burros in the area," he said. "Since the burros came here, they have run out the deer and are hard on bighorn sheep. And they damage the vegetation. Look out there at the palo verdes, even the ocotillos."

Dean Durfee, of the Phoenix office of the Bureau of Land Management, said research showed that the numbers of burros should be brought down.

"The purpose," he said, "is to reduce the number down to what the area will support, so we can continue having burros there. If we don't do something, the burros will eat themselves out of house and home."

Durfee said the 1971 Free Roaming Wild Horse and Burro Act allows reductions through relocating animals, capturing them, putting them up for adoption, and, as a last resort, using expert riflemen to destroy them.

Prescribed areas for relocation are either fully-obligated or over-obligated, Durfee said, but there is considerable interest in adopting out the number that can be practically captured. Regulations would be attached to adoptions.

"We plan on coming in there in May to capture burros in the Alamo Herd Management area," he said. "Some will be corralled on a ranch, some will be roped. We think we can catch 300 or so."

The captured burros will be moved to a central corral near Wenden where they will be offered to successful applicants under the BLM "Adopt a Burro" program. Responsible "foster parents" can adopt a wild burro at no charge, provided they can properly care for the animal and will not use it for any commercial purpose. In 1977, applications were available from the Arizona State office, Bureau of Land Management, 2400 Valley Bank Center, Phoenix, 85073.

Burros seek shade during the heat of the day and stay in the hills. They are hard to see because their color blends into the background. When the weather gets hotter, the burros come out of the hills in greater numbers for food and water.

Burros in the area, it was reported, are not apt to be aggressive unless a waterhole is involved. However, a burro bit one girl at the lake.

The Mike Flemmings of Phoenix were among the throng spending the night in the camp along the lake. Mrs. Flemming declared she heard burros "heehawing" in the night.

Some vacationers were hitching boats to vehicles for the return trip home. Others were sleeping or eating under improvised shelters. Radio music blared from a van, and a cruising boat left V-shape designs in its wake.

Despite 91-degree heat, it was comfortable in the shade. The park lies in the heart of one of Arizona's wide open spaces, the unspoiled **Bill Williams River Valley** in both Yuma and Mohave counties. The 500-acre lake is a good warm-weather fishery and rangers said the bass fishing is "picking up." They admonished visitors about rattle-snakes.

Facilities include primitive campsites, a trailer park with 19 hook-ups (sometimes difficult to get one), modern campsites, showers and a dump station. Water is available at the camp, but it is advisable for people to bring their own drinking water, a ranger said, if they have a low tolerance to minerals.

Alamo Lake's primary purpose is flood control, and the dam is controlled by the Army Corps of Engineers. The lake level varies after upstream rains.

Part of the lake covers the historical **Alamo Crossing.** Founded by Tom Rogers about the turn of the century, it served as a small mining community for transient prospectors.

For many years a five-stamp mill was used for custom milling at **Alamo Crossing.** In time, the ore supply from mines in the district was exhausted. The town revived briefly during the manganese boom in the early 1950s.

After visiting the lake, our party set out on a gravel road in the hills, hoping to see a burro. An old cottonwood tree not far from the Sandy River provided cool shade for a picnic.

A tour revealed clusters of yellow spring flowers, smoke trees and cholla and ocotillo cacti in bloom.

Back at the ranger station shortly after 5 p.m., we reported to a ranger that the burros were still elusive.

"You will see some if you stay around this evening," he promised. "Try **Spencer Draw** and take a drive back to the **Bill Williams Overlook.**

"Drive slowly, keep your windows down and you may hear them coming in from the hills," he said. "You may even see an all-white burro."

We cruised in the car, stopping to listen, but the only sound was a cricket. A soft breeze stirred the yellow flowers beside the road.

Finally, as the sun was descending, the Jeep rounded a curve in the road and there—down in a little draw—was a pack of six burros, one pure white.

The thrill—akin to discovery of a treasure—was big. Everyone cautiously bailed out from the car, but the burros picked up their ears, stared back, then began pulling away. Camera buffs had little chance to "shoot" their quarry.

Setting sail on Lake Alamo

To see things through the EAGLE'S EYE

A service station attendant here said that a beautiful view of the country could be gained by climbing to the **Eagle's Eye** in a mountain by that name south of **Aguila.**

"You can get up there through the draw beyond the cemetery," he said. "But watch out for rattlesnakes."

It was early in the morning and the **Eagle's Eye** seemed to fairly wink, beckoning a quartet of middle-aged climbers. Even from a distance, the climb seemed somewhat formidable.

"Well, let's just get a closer look," one said. "We can get a picture of the **Eagle's Eye** from a closer vantage point."

Our car nosed down a road heading straight south of **U.S. 60.** Alongside the neatly-kept cemetery, six miles south of here a cow trail led toward the base of **Eagle Eye Mountain.**

Stepping from the car, we scanned **Eagle Eye** and—well, one step just called for another. In no time we were up the draw, winding through blooming ocotillo and an assortment of mesquite and black boulders.

On the mountain between us and the **Eagle's Eye,** there was a strange outcropping with a huge loop hole. The sun beamed brighter, and it was obvious that the climb ahead was steep.

The four hikers huddled in conference, but the answer was already a foregone conclusion. We pushed onward and upward.

Climbing got steeper and steeper until progress was made by clutching to the rocks and ascending in a crouched position. Protecting cameras was a concern as rocks and stones skidded beneath the feet.

Once the first "loop-eye" was gained, all four climbers rested and admired the breath-taking panorama below. Cameras were aimed through and about the hole in the rock.

Studying the **Eagle-Eye** above, we decided on a second conference. With a ghost town miles beyond yet to explore and the hardship the climb ahead might impose, pursuit of that goal was abandoned. The descent was treacherous.

My helpmate volunteered to carry my camera on his back to save it from banging against the rocks. The camera case, of course, had been left at home.

Everything went fine until he stumbled and fell backwards—on top of the camera. Fortunately injuries were minor to both.

Once again on level terrain, we all felt a sense of achievement with pictures safely in the camera.

But back in the car, smugness was dispelled. The camera jammed on the rewind. When it was opened, seven pictures from the heart of the film roll were lost.

That, more than the rigors of the climb, took the starch out of the climbers.

Eagle's Eye view

EAGLE TAIL MOUNTAINS
—pictographs of long ago!

A search for ancient pictography near **Harquahala** is a rewarding experience.

The bonanza in pictographs—pictures scrawled on rocks — appeared after a grueling drive on the backside of the **Eagle Tail Mountains.**

The quest began when we arrived at the Herb Harris home near **Tonopah.**

"The Eagle Tail Mountains are so-named because they are the tail of a range of mountains that, from a very high distance, have the appearance of an eagle," Harris explained.

Six persons with picnic supplies then loaded the Jeep Wagoneer to head into the Eagle Tails.

The first landmark commanding the view was the picturesque **Court House Rock.** For a time, travel was on a gas pipe line route. There were sundry dips and washes and the trail veered to the back of the mountain range.

The desert was green, purple and beige in the early light—ocotillos, stately cacti, paloverdes fresh-washed by rain, mountain peaks and greasewood galore.

The trail took a turn for the worse. The driver switched into four-wheel drive to tackle the jolting, jostling, rocky, one-car-width trail that meshed into a steep mountain wash.

Harris, who had been in the area years before, became the navigator. He advised when to veer left or swing right to dodge rocks and avoid "high center" scrunches.

For a time there was the security of another four-wheeler on the trail. The two men ahead were seeking quail and deer.

Clean air and remoteness were other attractions of the boondock area.

"It's so wild in here that snakes eat mustard in the wintertime," Harris quipped. He told tales of mines and water potholes in the mountain recesses.

Finally, the bad part of the trail was behind and the good news —the picture rocks—appeared.

Everyone bailed out of the vehicle. No one really wanted to acknowledge, though, that clouds were assembling.

Most picture writings, of course, were in the higher reaches of the mountains, and the scramble amid the black sharp rocks for closeup looks was earnest.

Some long ago generation—no one present could even guess at the tribe—chronicled events on the rocks. It was engaging to check the variety—goats, crosses, a wheel divided into seven parts, something that looked like "rain coming down," flowers and geometric designs.

In a few places, there was modern day graffiti. Also on the scene were millipedes and a huge, clumsy tarantula. But, they were for real.

Clouds thickened and the rough trail back had to be traversed immediately.

Four-wheel drive vehicle noses up jolting trail.

THE WHITE TANKS
your neighborhood waterfalls!

Harbingers of spring were emerging on a January morning in the **White Tanks Mountain Park,** one of Maricopa County's most inviting areas.

Already there were tiny flowers strewn at random and grass carpets beneath the palo verde. Birds sang and chipmunks darted across desert trails.

A herd of deer hid in the mountain recesses, and a sign beckoned hardy visitors to a mountain waterfall trail.

The park's elevation provides a scenic overlook of the Valley. Concrete picnic tables and benches sit among the cactus, sagebrush and mesquite trees.

The top drawing card, however, is the abundance of petroglyphs. The inscribed, black-faced rocks give visitors an insight into mankind centuries ago.

The park is reached by heading west on Olive Avenue from Grand Avenue, some 16 miles to the entrance.

According to Erv Hiser, park manager, the park, about 26,300 acres in size, is the largest in the county system.

"It's a good place for birders, too," Hiser said. "Hawks, several varieties of cactus wrens, cardinals, Gila woodpeckers, and red-shafted thrashers are among the bird population."

It is believed that the Hohokam Indians stopped and camped for a time in the White Tanks. The petroglyphs attest to the level of their culture. Chances are slim, however, of spying a pottery shard or arrowhead.

Indian artifacts are protected. It is against state, federal and county laws to remove them. Vandals, however, have taken a toll.

"We need more groups like Scouts and Audubon societies. It helps cut down on vandalism when 'square' citizens are around," Hiser said. Visitors are advised to lock their cars before walking the trail to the waterfall.

The waterfall trail that winds by the petroglyphs dissipates among huge boulders. At the top of the boulder area and beneath towering cliffs is a water basin. The basin is fed by a waterfall activated by rain and seepage from above. During last year's winter wet season, the waterfall became tremendous, Hiser said.

The cliffs are dangerous to climb. Two people were killed climbing there last year, and already this year (in 1980) there has been a serious accident. Hiser wishes there were a way to convince people not to climb the dangerous cliffs.

There are areas in the park for overnight camping, for small fees.

"Small game hunting is permitted outside the developed area of the park, but big game hunting is prohibited," the ranger said.

Work on trails and other park facilities was underway by the Young Adult Conservation Corps in a government-sponsored program.

The **White Tanks Mountains** are so named because of the granite boulders, mostly white, in washes that often hold water. From the air, the basins have the appearance of white tanks.

The quiet desert beauty offers a retreat from the valley's hustle and bustle without denting a gasoline budget too deeply.

Park Manager indicates ancient writings.

PALM CANYON
fronds on the desert!

The palm-filled wedge towering on the wall of the **Kofa Mountains' Palm Canyon** dazzled like an oasis in the sky.

Glimmering bright green in a canyon within a canyon, the palms hung, to the eye of the beholder, like a picture of awesome beauty, wedged in the stark, slab-faced mountains.

The sheer phenomenon of the wild palms in the unusual habitat beckoned and challenged. Our party had breakfasted early in **Wickenburg,** then headed west on the California highway to **Quartzsite.** Knowing that the sun would shine on the palm cleft around the noon-tide, we had budgeted our time accordingly.

At **Quartzsite,** we headed south 19 miles on **U.S. 95** and found the graveled trail leading into the **Kofa National Wildlife Refuge** with **Palm Canyon** clearly marked. Except for sharp dips, which we navigated cautiously, the nine-mile trail was not too bad.

The huge refuge of 666,000 acres of pristine desert contains old mine sites, including the most notable—the **King of Arizona Mine,** operated early in the century. The mine gave the mountains their name—**Kofa** being a contraction of "King of Arizona."

The environment is the home of desert bighorn sheep as well as the California Palm, rated the only native palm in Arizona. It is the west end of the **Kofa Mountains** that is well known for the palms in the spectacular setting.

Amid a profusion of cholla cactus, the ocotillos were bursting into red bloom and the greasewood was in yellow blossom. The **Kofa Mountains** as they loomed nearer were wildly rugged. The drive ended near the entrance of the canyon.

After a half-mile hike, we were within spectator distance of the main grove of palms, high on the north canyon wall. Their beauty was rewarding, and more palms peeked from other areas of the canyon.

Our venturesome party agreed unanimously to climb to the main grove. We were forewarned that the climb up the narrow cleft was rugged and should be tackled only by the hale and hearty. Later, we said "amen" to this advice and labeled the stint hazardous.

The climb called for figuring where to put your feet and hands next, alertness for sliding rocks, a wary eye and ear for rattlesnakes. Not until we emerged through a steep slot were the palms again visible.

All of us panted as we heaved ourselves up through the slot, but imediately the struggle was eclipsed by the spectacle of the palms. The rustle of the palm fronds in the cool breeze was refreshing as we rested and waited for the sun to fully bathe the grove.

Wonder spot—first vista of palms

One botanist, judging that the patch of palms may have been growing for centuries in the canyon, said that droppings of birds containing seeds from California trees may explain their existence in this place. How the palms, termed *Washingtonia filiferas,* received nourishment from the apparently soil-less crack in the volcanic formation and the apparent lack of moisture were other wonderments.

Many of the tall palms were blackened by a fire set in 1954 by either carelessness or vandalism. The trees were again thriving, and occasionally there were wild flowers in the grove.

Back down on the floor of the main canyon, we were thankful for the safe trip. While a hummingbird flitted about a flowering tree in the remote solitude, we watched the palm picture in the tall reaches of the canyon with new appreciation.

* * * * *

Addendum: The above story, written in 1966, records success in reaching the towering canyon. But, in a return effort in 1980, we were unable to reach the pocket of palms.

Almost within a stone's throw from our objective, a naked rock, gargantuan in size, proved a formidable barrier. Perhaps more experienced climbers with proper equipment could negotiate the climb. Our fear was that if we succeeded in surmounting the rock we could not get down again.

Reluctantly, we inched our way back down—sometimes by the seat of our trousers. Perhaps, the better part of valor really is discretion.

Back on the main path, we paused to view the palms in their lofty perch. The sight from the safer vantage point was reward enough.

Oasis amid huge stones in Kofa Mountains

PAINTED ROCKS PARK
petroglyphs of the past!

Looking for some good reading—something novel, in big type?

An eye-catching collection of unique stories tucked away in a remote area may be the venturesome answer. The manuscript has not achieved the bestseller list—and the writing, admittedly, is hard to understand. Besides, no one knows exactly who the author or authors were.

But, if the test of good literature is time—these epics must be a success. Some of the writings may be 1,000 years old.

Interested?

Well, it takes a little doing and time to get there. And a jigger of climbing. And, for the most enjoyment, the weather should be cool. Take along a sack lunch because this open-air library has picnic facilities.

The "library" is amidst huge black basalt boulders in the **Painted Rocks State Historic Park.** The location is in Maricopa County, 15 miles west of **Gila Bend** on Interstate 8, then north 12 miles from a well-marked turnoff. All but less than a mile of the road is paved.

Although the park is named for the etchings, it is obvious that the rock designs are not paintings as the name implies. It is thought, however, that most etchings were also painted. Similar etchings have been found in more protected areas along the Gila River that contain paint chips within them, a park paper notes.

There are many theories why the Hohokams chose the particular

Ancient petroglyphs pique visitors' interest.

rock mound in the park for their art work. The two most widely accepted are that the area was a meeting place for trading with other people, and for unknown reasons, was held sacred.

A park sign notes that the meaning of the petroglyphs is known only to those who made them. Yet, the writings pique the interest and fancy of 20th Century travelers. The picture rocks were set apart as a 20-acre state park in 1965.

The Indian rock-art drawings are of lizards, men, geometric figures and unidentified squiggles.

The unusual scene was mentioned by Father Kino in 1699 and earned diary entries by scores of '49ers, immigrants and passengers on the Butterfield Stage.

Construction of **Painted Rock Dam,** some 181 feet high and located about four miles away, was completed in November, 1959. The dam, built to retard not store water, is a flood-control project designed to protect sections of irrigated land in Arizona, California and Mexico.

Painted Rock Park facilities include two large ramadas, primitive campsites and chemical toilets. No water is available. Elevation is 735 feet. A sign notes nominal fees for use of the state park.

Armando Vasquez, ranger assistant, says there are probably 8,000 to 10,000 visitors a year to the park. The park is well kept and includes little paths among the picture rocks, a cactus garden, palo verde trees and greasewood. Surrounding hills add other color notes.

The old Butterfield Southern Overland Mail Co. Stage route is said to have passed directly in front of the picture rocks.

And to add extra atmosphere, the notorious Oatman Massacre in 1851, in which a family of nine were waylaid by Indians, occurred about four miles west of the petroglyphs. Two girls survived and were sold as slaves. Olive Oatman was rescued in 1856. Her sister died in captivity.

More good "reading" at Painted Rock Park

In a cemetery near AJO—
epitaph written in copper wire

What may be the most unusual tombstone in Arizona—it has an epitaph almost 400 words long—is located in the old cemetery near **Ajo.**

The words are fashioned out of copper wire and are embedded on a stone cross that stands six feet high, exclusive of an 18-inch base.

Charles D. Dunn of **Phoenix** knows the story of the headstone because he helped make it.

He said work on the tombstone began in 1933 when he was hired for 50 cents an hour by a friend, Frank Randall, to assist in making the headstone for the late husband of Mrs. Lewis Conde of **Ajo.**

Mrs. Conde, widowed two years, disdained smooth, ordinary monuments. The monument for her husband, apparently a spiritualist minister, must be a cross, a "rugged one," she said.

Dunn said he and Randall trucked peacock copper rock from the **Bloody Basin** and **Copper Basin** areas to a backyard workshop on Henshaw Road (now Buckeye Road).

They obtained the wire for the inscription from the old Central Arizona Power Co. As they fashioned the wire with pliers into inch-tall letters, each was soldered to a nail, later to be embedded in the concrete face of the cross.

Dunn said Mrs. Conde came periodically to the work scene with more words for the epitaph.

He said when the inscription kept getting longer and longer, he and Randall reduced the size of the letters. Dunn said they were paid for their work once a week in cash.

Randall also hired another man to assist and, after three months, Dunn returned to a forestry service job. The monument was still not completed.

"When it was completed," said Dunn, "Randall loaded the cross, weighing about a ton, and took it to **Ajo.** I never saw him again."

Fifteen years later, curiosity took Dunn to the cemetery to see if he could locate the cross. He found it on the west side of the cemetery.

The Epitaph reads in part:

Lahissa, Lewis Conde, 18— to 1931. For all races, people, beliefs. He came, and they knew him not. Actuated by the spirit that has guided all teachers, he came to lead human beings into a new era . . . The era of man's full consciousness of the power within him . . .

Man's power is unlimited . . . and can reach out and get what he wants from that unusual mind. He came to overcome the so-called laws of nature. He will go around the earth in a flash of a moment and

Unusual tombstone near Ajo

to the planets . . .

Each one is a spoke in a wheel leading to the center—Give the best in you, this way you will find happiness—Indeed, Lahissa showed the way. He lived all phases and mastered all conditions—was persecuted and prosecuted. The foundation has been laid. It is left to others to bring into being the brotherhood of man—

(In a 1981 check, the unique tombstone still stands tall in the cemetery)

The whence and whither of WHY

Relatively few people know the where, when, what and why of **Why,** a tiny community south of **Ajo** at the junction of **Arizona 85** and **86.**

But Peggy Kater, sometimes called the "mayor" of **Why,** knows the answers.

Mrs. Kater came to **Why** in 1949 with her late husband, James C. Kater. That was after she got the Bureau of Land Management to open up a few tracts of land around **Why.**

A former trader, trapper and gold miner on the nearby Papago Indian Reservation, Mrs. Kater was a mover in developing the area and naming the town, which has a population of 130 (in 1979).

"The place used to be called **Rocky Point Junction** (because it was the turning point enroute to **Rocky Point,** Mexico), but when folks here got ready for a post office, the postal department said there were too many junctions.

"So we had a meeting. Because so many people asked why anyone would come out here, we all decided that **Why** would be a good name," she explained.

Main Street in remote Why

The Katers had built a bar, cafe, store and post office. Water was brought in from **Ajo,** but as more people came, a well was developed with federal funds. Another major project, bringing in electricity, was accomplished.

During this time, many older folks, not very well-to-do, parked their trailers at what is now a highway rest area. Many of them hoped to stay in **Why** permanently.

But the county health department, noting the lack of sanitary facilities, decided the campers must go.

"They were on limited Social Security and most couldn't afford commercial trailer court rentals," said Mrs. Kater. "Some permanent residents and I applied to the Bureau of Land Management for 122 acres of ground for a trailer court and camp ground. We got a special dispensation from the health department if we could install a park in 30 days.

"At that time (about 1970)," she continued, "there were about 63 people living here permanently. Almost everyone pitched in. One man provided heavy machinery, others the labor. Those too old to do heavy labor cooked stew and chili beans for workers," Mrs. Kater said.

There were other benefit events, but in 30 days, the park was ready. It boasted roads, restrooms and hot water for showers. The water-lines were dug by women and children.

The non-profit park was named "Coyote Howls."

Most residents move out during the hot summer months, but some stay all year. Payment per month depends on whether occupants are over or under 62. There are also daily and weekly rates. The park is administered by the Why Utility Co. and everyone who has a meter is a member of the corporation, Mrs. Kater said.

At night, park people gather 'round campfires and exchange stories. "You can really get an education hearing gossip from all over the country," Mrs. Kater said.

After there was a park, the people needed a place to meet. So they banded together to get the community center.

Mrs. Kater later sold the bar and store and developed Pozo Redondo Park, which also has electricity and water facilities.

Coyote Park people feed quail and birds. Sometimes a gray fox meanders through the area and the peace and quiet is disturbed only when coyotes turn over garbage cans.

And, yes, the coyotes do howl at night.

(A visit to **Why** might be combined with a visit to **Organ Pipe Cactus National Monument** a short distance south from **Why** on **State 85.** In **Ajo,** also on **State 85,** there are motels.)

ORGAN PIPE NATIONAL MONUMENT

The **Sonoran Desert** reflecting changing moods and colors and a myriad of cacti combine to make a fascinating sojourn in the **Organ Pipe National Monument.**

The park is in its wintertime best, carpeted with rain-prompted grass and backgrounded with purple-hued mountains.

Arizona 85, south of **Ajo,** cuts a scenic swath through the monument.

Visitors were delighted last weekend (in February) with an unusual fringe benefit on the **Ajo Mountain Drive** within the monument. An expanse of spring poppies on a hillside provided an eye-catching vista.

The "orange cloud," a considerable distance from the road, challenged this reporter and her husband for a closeup look. After lunch near the **Diablo Wash,** we took off down one wash and up another, climbing at times in the grueling (for us) hike.

It seemed we would never get there, but the effort proved rewarding. The poppies at close range were a brilliant color bonanza.

Resting back at the picnic site, it was novel to watch the out-of-state cars cruise by with passengers craning their necks to absorb the scenery. The out-of-staters ranged from Delaware and New York to Oregon and Ontario.

For first timers in the monument, there is a choice of making the 51-mile **Puerto Blanco Drive,** which includes the **Quitobaquito** pond, or the 21-mile **Ajo Mountain Drive.** Hardy souls with enough time might elect to make both drives. Since our party had traveled the **Puerto Blanco Drive** several years ago, we opted for the shorter trek.

It's a good idea to stop first at the visitor's center, where booklets are available for each drive. The booklets describe the areas as marked by numbered stakes. One member of our party read aloud the corresponding descriptions, adding depth and education to the trip.

The booklet also lists words of caution about such things as desert washes and reminds visitors not to get "too familiar with the cactus, especially the jumping cholla."

Best chances of seeing wildlife are in early morning and late afternoon hours. It may be because of the cold nights, but no snakes were seen on the February trip.

There are four areas with picnic tables and ramadas. Fires are not permitted and water is not available, the booklet reminds.

Natural arch

The **Ajo Mountain Drive** winds eastward through hills and valleys in a colorful part of the monument. The desert is a vast and unusual place where plants and animals flourish.

Among desert flora, to name a few, are ocotillo, palo verde, creosote bush, chain-fruit cholla, prickly pear and barrel cactus, mesquite and ironwood trees, jojoba, Mexico jumping bean and Christmas cactus.

Obviously, the tour offers a field day for camera buffs. One point of interest is the "Natural Arch—37 feet high, 90 feet wide and more than 720 feet above the roadway." It was formed by erosive forces, and eventually the rock became thin. Weaker parts collapsed, creating the arch.

A cactus confrontation

A blanket of Mexican goldpoppies

48   ORGAN PIPE (Southwest Arizona)

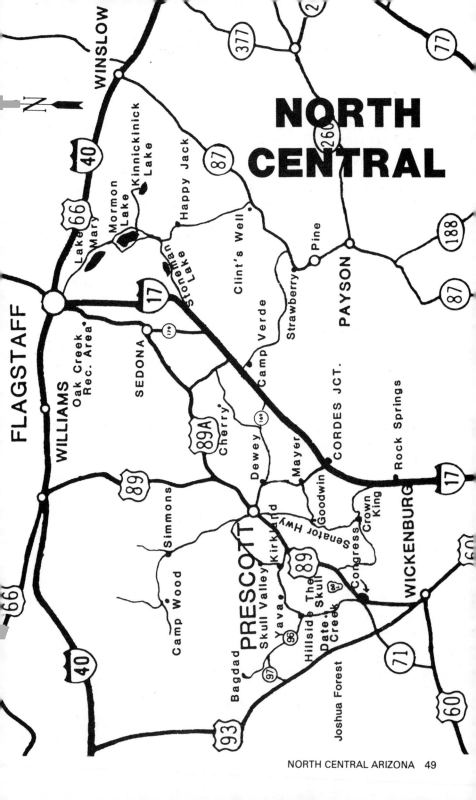

NORTH CENTRAL

THE BAGDAD SWING
—historic, scenic central Arizona

A trip through Arizona's midsection brings the traveler to the **Joshua Forest,** to pine country and to a number of interesting mountain villages.

The junket, pleasant in the spring, includes **Bagdad, Hillside, Yava, Kirkland,** and **Skull Valley. Prescott** is reached either by the paved road through **Iron Springs** or a dirt road through **Copper Basin Canyon.**

Among the scenery are the **Santa Maria River, Kirkland Creek,** quaint windmills, yellow flowers and historic old buildings in unexpected places.

Our cross-section tour left **U.S. 93** (the **Kingman highway**) on paved **Arizona 97** to **Bagdad,** through palo verde and cactus-clad hills.

The road to **Bagdad** junctions with **Arizona 96** for a short stretch into **Bagdad** and dead-ends near the Cyprus Bagdad Copper Co. open pit mine. Our stop at the scale office for permission to peek at the mine was rewarded with hard hats and instructions to reach the viewpoint.

"You can pick up a few rocks near the viewpoint," advised an attendant. By midmorning, rock collectors were already on hand at the rock pile, digging, browsing and searching for the bright turquoise-colored chunks. (The mine, however, closed in 1984.)

Open pit copper mine

Nostalgic depot at Hillside

Hillside, some 23 miles from **Bagdad** on **Arizona 96,** was drowsing in the noon sun, with only a few of its residents in evidence. The **Hillside** store is a monument to the past, with the "1885" date painted boldly across the outside.

Mrs. Kenneth (Garna) Walker, a **Hillside** resident for 11 years, was posting letters at the village "post office"—a string of mail boxes served by a rural carrier between **Prescott** and **Bagdad.**

The post office was established in **Hillside** in 1888, and in 1904 a Wells Fargo station was opened.

The freight train that hauls for the Cyprus Bagdad mine, the E.J. Dickie Trucking Co. and area ranchers give the community extra life.

Mrs. Walker pointed with pride to the Hillside Bible Church completed more than a year ago.

She drives the bus for the school, which now boasts two rooms and two teachers.

"I like the quietness here, the people, the lack of hustle and bustle," Mrs. Walker said. "And, it's home."

At the little red depot, a dog stood guard in the doorway.

Sprawling ranches dotted the scenery enroute to **Kirkland.** Two teenage girls were wading in **Kirkland Creek** at **Yava.**

Kirkland was named for William J. Kirkland, who came to Arizona in 1856. He and his wife were said to be the first "American" couple married in Arizona. They moved to **Kirkland** in 1863.

Today, there's a cluster of buildings, including a bar and a little post office. The post office front room bore wallpaper with a Bicentenial design.

Skull Valley, seven miles away, lay peacefully in the March sun, a far cry from events that led to its name. It is said that when the first white man entered the valley, he found piles of bleached Indian skulls. Some historians say the skulls were the result of fights between Apaches and Maricopas.

The **Copper Basin road** takes off near the Skull Valley Community Church for those who want to tackle the more adventuresome route to **Prescott**. The road in higher reaches is not wide enough for two cars, as it winds through scenic forest areas.

In higher altitudes, there were patches of snow. The forest stillness was broken by the sound of water from springs and melting snow.

With an early morning start, the trip from **Phoenix** can be made in a day. A hearty breakfast in **Wickenburg** is fun, and, for extra zest, a picnic lunch can be brought.

Copper Basin Road in the forest primeval

CAMP WOOD ADVENTURE
a backwoods road; an old cemetery

Adventurers who like their travel rugged and away from crowds will find a special swath in the Prescott National Forest rewarding.

The backwoodsy road may be reached by taking the **Miller Valley Road** out of **Prescott,** then turning onto the **Simmons** and **Camp Wood Road.** The trail snakes through juniper, manzanita and white flower vistas before verging into the heavy-scented pines.

The sometimes rough and narrow road country boasts ranger stations and an old fort site, shaded picnic areas and a measure of history.

All this and a quiet interrupted by chirping birds and sighing pines, plus quail and squirrels that scamper across the road. In a real delight, a deer boldly watched our approaching car before scampering deep into the forest.

Picnic supplies should be adequate. The forest was fire-warning dry during our visit and it was well our picnic fare was ready-to-eat.

Camp Wood was only a shadow of its former days. The old school house had been vacated since the mid-Sixties and the post office no longer existed. History notes the area was settled as early as 1880 and first called **Kymo.**

In the early 1890's a cavalry captain named Wood is said to have camped here during a scouting expedition and the area gradually became known as **Camp Wood.** Still others say that a former sawmill was a key factor to the camp.

The place now is devoted to the ranger station. Ranger Ron Melcher was helpful, sketching a map and directing our party to Walnut Creek station, **Camp Hualapai** and an old cemetery. He quoted an epitaph on an old tombstone and warned about rattlesnakes.

The rough road wound past rustic corrals, grazing light-colored cattle, a ranch or two, and through creek beds, washes and shallow pools.

Walnut Creek Ranger Station was canopied in giant walnut trees and there were few reminders of the past at **Camp Hualapai.**

A sign noted that General George Crook commanded a military post there 1869-1873. Its mission was to protect travelers using the toll road running from **Fort Whipple** to the Colorado River.

An old cemetery with rotting picket fences around the graves contained tombstones dating back to the 1890's. In tribute to Marilla Jane Rogers who died in 1897, an inscription on a headboard above her tombstone said:

"With this grave an angel lies, no myth that flits above the skies. A host in life of friendly ties, bespoke an angel good and wise."

Camp Hualapai complete with old-fashioned stile

THE SKULL
relic of a tall tale!

The Skull, a little known Arizona landmark, stares enigmatically at passersby on a dusty gravel road to **Date Creek.**

Few people know its real history, but Lee R. Roberts, a Phoenician, put an inquirer on the right track. He was a conductor on the Santa Fe passenger train that once plied the rails between **Phoenix** and **Prescott.**

The Skull was an attraction for easterners on the train, and Roberts, known for his jovial patter, played the saga to the hilt. Passengers ate up the story, realizing it was a bit of skullduggery.

Roberts believes the Santa Fe originally painted the mammoth rock in a likeness of a skull. He retired in 1968 and the passenger train was withdrawn in 1969. The Santa Fe, which still hauls freight over the line, apparently lost interest in refurbishing **The Skull.**

"When I was six years old, mother took me on my first train ride — from **Wickenburg** to **Prescott,**" Roberts said. "I remember seeing the skull then. Right now I'm 86. As far as I know it has been painted 80 years."

Later, as conductor, Roberts hatched up a wild story to tell passengers as the train approached **The Skull,** about an Indian scout, who dealt misery and death to other Indians.

The train left **Phoenix** at 4 p.m., and Roberts would tell the tale as the train came up through **Martinez Valley.** A few minutes ahead of **The Skull,** Roberts told passengers to look to the right to see the skull of the Indian scout, "just as the Indians went off and left him way back in 1860.

"Of course their mouths were all open," Roberts continued. "It just so happens that, going north, there is a little point in the mountains and **The Skull** is behind it. They couldn't see it until they were right on it. They'd all cross over to one side of the train to look. When the train whipped around the corner, there was **The Skull.**"

And gasps from the passengers!

Roberts, earlier had told passengers the legend of the **Hassayampa River**—about how people didn't tell the truth after drinking its water.

"After **The Skull,** passengers would say, 'well, Old Boy, you sure drank too much of that water'," said Roberts, chuckling.

Actually, as Roberts stated, nature dropped two large rocks in the shape of a "V" and dropped into it another large rock in the shape of a skull.

"At one time the Santa Fe had a paint gang that moved about in outfit cars," the Phoenician said. "They repainted mileposts and signs

on bridges. When they were in that neighborhood, they painted **The Skull.**"

The way to the skull is through mountain and desert scenery. Take-off point beyond **Congress** on **U.S. 89** is a gravel road to the west, marked simply by a sign, **"Date Creek** and **Hillside."**

The dusty road skirts and crosses the Santa Fe Railroad tracks. The road is washboardy, full of dips. Signs, "Trapline Danger" and "No Trespassing" are in evidence.

The place of **The Skull,** about 6.3 miles from the turnoff, was off the road a distance beyond the railroad and fence, and can be seen from the roadway.

Not far from the skull rock is **Date Creek,** a ranch and green meadow.

SENATOR HIGHWAY
Prescott to Crown King

Spectacular scenery is a bonus for those who take a trip back into history on the old **Senator Highway** in Yavapai County.

The 41-mile-long pioneer pathway winds through ponderosa pine, fir, oak, willow, aspen, sumac and prickly pear cactus.

And for history buffs, sparse remnants of the mining-linked communities of **Maxton, Goodwin, Venezia** and **Senator** offer a nostalgic trip in time.

The original road, built in segments according to the vagaries of mining development, was constructed about 100 years ago. Today's road is said to follow basically the same route. The **Senator Mine,** for which the **Senator Camp** and the road apparently were named, was in existence as early as 1878.

Our party of four left **Prescott** early to enjoy a full day on the road, have a leisurely lunch and photograph the sights.

The **Senator Highway,** which can be reached by taking Prescott's South Mount Vernon Street, is paved as far as **Groom Creek.**

At **Groom Creek,** a bulletin board notice caused a conference. Public health authorities, it stated among other information, had determined that "bubonic plague is present in rats and rodents in Yavapai County." With no pets along and the firm intention of staying clear of such varmints we proceeded.

The road was dusty, riddled with potholes and bumpy, criss-crossed at times with little streams, certainly no place for cars with low clearance. The one-lane road dished out a few hair-raisers, such as the time we had to back up the mountain road to let another car pass. Wet seasons would preclude travel on the trail.

At **Maxton,** which is marked by a collapsed building, we took a one-mile side trip up the **Walker Road** to visit the old **Pickerill Mill** and the **Hassayampa Lake** and dam. Quaking aspens, pines and the moon still visible in the late morning sky made a great scene.

Back on the **Senator** and past **Storm Cloud Mill,** the grueling grind began up **Mount Union.** At times, old oaks arched over the trail.

We failed to find **Crook City,** with its two wells, but **White's Well** (not for drinking) was near the roadside.

Venezia, where historians say gold was milled for mines in **Crooks Canyon,** proved a favorite. Part of the 20-stamp mill remains, but it was a bevy of fragrant wild pink roses that captured our fancy. Dense shade and a breeze rustling through the pines provided a perfect setting for our picnic.

Palace Station was a pleasant stop. The cabin, built in the 1870s, is now a U.S. Forest Service ranger station occupied (in 1978) by Douglas Vandergon and his wife, Susan, two large dogs and a cat named Wallaby. The couple was married on the front porch of the cabin.

Their cabin is without electricity, so the couple cooks on a wood stove. A propane refrigerator is one of their few luxuries.

"We like living here," said Mrs. Vandergon. She keeps a calendar, noting activities, rainfall measurements, and the number of vehicles going by (by noon our car was the 20th). She drives to **Prescott** periodically to pick up mail and supplies, reads classics and Westerns and tends her summer garden.

After leaving the station, our travel slowed at times to 10 mph or less, due to the rough road. Once cattle with numbered tags dangling from their ears blocked our way.

The road forked to **Mayer,** but we chose the route to **Crown King** to continue on the **Senator Highway.**

Soon after passing an old corral where **Arrastra** and **Turkey Creeks** join, we tackled the last and roughest lap to **Crown King.**

The sun was casting long shadows when we finally left **Crown King** on the road to **Interstate 17.**

... not suited for passenger cars

CHERRY—
an old schoolhouse restored!

On the far southeast slope of **Mingus Mountain,** this once-thriving hub of mining now boasts a population fluctuating around 50, a converted vintage school house, an antique shop, and a former stagecoach station.

Nearby, **Powell Springs** campground, 5,252 feet high in the pine scented forest, offers a chance to picnic and relax.

Dr. Mary Maher, a former Phoenix College faculty member, is delighted to be living in a house that served from 1884 to 1943 as the **Cherry** school house. She bought it in 1970. The tab was $650.

"The old schoolhouse was just a shell. I had my eye on it about 10 years," Ms. Maher said. "The basic structure was sound, but the roof was gone. Some neighbors thought it should be torn down and taken to the dump."

Instead, she realized her vision of redoing the structure. Several thousand dollars and much time later, she had a unique house with fireplace. The television antenna is attached to the pole that long ago was used for playground equipment.

The house, though, retains its schoolhouse character.

"There's nothing like it," Ms. Maher said. "It's great to live here. And it is nostalgic to think I have the old schoolhouse. I've been told that during the gold-mining years there were about 35 students at the school. About 3,000 people lived here before we went off the gold standard."

At the Cherry Antique Shop, there's a little bit of most everything —even furniture. One shopper bought a small 1932 flag, a 1910 book and set of doll dishes.

Another shopper was delighted to purchase a collectable, 1976 Bicentennial year water glass, complete with Liberty Bell insignia and, of all things, a "Barry" political button that depicted a pair of blackrimmed glasses.

The R. W. Kenneys have operated the shop 17 years.

Cherry is 15 miles east of **Dewey,** on the **Cordes Junction-Prescott** road, and along **State Route 169.** About nine miles east, a sign indicates a turnoff on a gravel road the next six miles into **Cherry.** The winding road is crisscrossed with tiny streams. **Powell Springs** basked in a scenic wooded area a short distance from **Cherry.**

Several families, mostly members of the Rolling Hogan Club, were relaxed in their campers and trailers on the first day of summer.

The pines and wild grape vines were fragrant, and a murmuring stream added charm. A concrete table and benches beneath a canopy

Former stagecoach stop at old Cherry

of pine tree shade set the scene for picnic fare. A word to the wise: **don't forget insect repellent**.

In **Cherry,** Ms. Maher gave permission to enter the old cemetery where the oldest headstone was dated 1898.

Jerry Doyle, a Phoenix architect, and Dennis Wells, an engineer, gained a chunk of unique Arizona history when they acquired the fragile old stage stop in 1974.

Moved several hundred feet from its original stand but on the same homestead, the place was named to the State Register of Historic Places on Dec. 9, 1976.

Doyle said the home belonged to Richard Dekuhns and was in existence in 1878. Among its roles, the building was a home, post office and remount stop along the military road between **Fort Whipple** and **Fort Verde.**

A reporter from the ***Prescott Journal Miner*** in 1903 wrote about the comfortable house where the Dekuhns had lived at that time more than 25 years. The historic place at the time of our visit was under restoration and not open to the public.

Visitors here have the option of returning to **Phoenix** the easier way via **Dewey** or continuing east on the road that ends near **Camp Verde.** The rugged, sometimes eroded gravel road, requires close driving attention, but a fringe benefit is the lofty view of **Camp Verde** in the distance.

The red rock by-way to FLAGSTAFF

A bi-way route to **Flagstaff** in the summertime offers a change of scenery and a versatile vacationette.

The junket, in lieu of the fast-wheeling freeway, can be stretched to include the adventure of an overnight campout at one of the several campgrounds or, if the budget allows, a night in a **Flagstaff** motel.

The journey, including the bonus scenery of the return trip through **Oak Creek Canyon** and the majestic red rock country of **Sedona**, can be covered in a day.

The route, after the preliminary trip from **Phoenix** to **Payson**, swings through the beautiful **Mogollon Rim** country, **Pine, Strawberry, Clint's Well, Happy Jack, Mormon Lake** and **Lake Mary.**

A prepared picnic lunch is advisable, since the lunch hour may find the family in an area remote from restaurants, and fire danger in the forests is often extreme.

Out of **Sunflower,** century plants, towering like sentinels, were in golden bloom. At **Pine,** a quaint mountain village, a handhewn log house, built in 1889, was fronted with a graceful peach tree, pink hollyhocks and tinkling bells. The owner reported that the adjacent log house, where he maintains a blacksmith shop, was built in 1876. An old wagon, which brought "the Jones family" from Utah to

A house of yesteryear, built in 1876

Mormon Lake in quiet serenity

Arizona 100 years ago, and a vintage springboard wagon were among the storybook items.

At **Strawberry,** so named because wild strawberries once grew in the area, the road forks over **Strawberry Hill** and through the **Mogollon Rim** country to **Clint's Well.** The pine-and-oak-studded mountains were sparked with brilliant red and yellow wildflowers. Chipmunks darted across the road, and the air was clean and pine-scented.

Vacationers were enjoying the campsite at **Clint's Well,** where the road again forks, with the graded gravel road to **Flagstaff** on the left. Along the road, shared with logging trucks, signs told of such remote places as **Bald Mesa, Iron Mine Draw, Stoneman's Lake, Willow Valley** and **Turkey Mountain.**

At **Happy Jack,** a logging camp for about 300 residents, the U.S. flag was a bright note over the little post office. Huge logging trucks, loaded with heavy cargo, were ready to roll.

The resumption of pavement was welcomed about 6 miles south of **Mormon Lake.**

At **Lake Mary,** a sailing boat slithered quietly on the glistening lake. Young and old were casting for fish, and on the banks others lazed in the shade, relaxing in slow-gaited life.

OAK CREEK
west fork wilderness

Ranger Dan Wilson, piloting our hiking party to the well-defined path in the wilderness along the west fork of **Oak Creek,** predicted the "most beautiful walk of your life" ahead.

Wilson, of the Coconino National Forest staff, was not kidding.

Every bend in the path through the fern-carpeted forest was a vista of unspoiled beauty. The trail, always within listening of the murmuring creek, was an adventure, a joy.

The nature research area is relatively little known, since for many

Hikers ponder path of creek bed route.

Lodge hideaway

years the privately owned Mayhew Lodge stood virtually in the mouth of the west fork. The only access, Wilson said, was a small corridor. The Mayhew Oak Creek Lodge was destroyed by fire in 1980.

There are no roads in the wilderness, which is restricted—no camping, campfires or motor vehicles. Ruggedness keeps remote areas somewhat closed, but there are several crossings of the west fork area within its easier accessible areas. In the upper recesses, the river has waist-high pockets.

Twelve hundred plants and trees have been identified in the canyon. Sycamore, box elder, willow, maple, Douglas and white firs, ponderosa pine and the lacy leaf juniper mark the forest. There's a scattering of blackberries and raspberries, moss galore, and wild grapevines climb among the trees.

Then there are "scads of violets," as Wilson put it, jack-in-the-pulpit, ladies' slippers, and many other flowers in a rainbow of colors. There is also poison ivy.

Asked about the wildlife, Wilson's remark added zest: "You might look for black bear. There's evidence—the bark has been scratched off some trees."

With that, our party of four took off rapidly down the trail. Frank Barker and his wife, Georgia, made the jaunt in training for an intended hike across one of the Hawaiian Islands. Frank carried a backpack loaded with lunches and beverages for four, and other gear.

Past the fifth crossing (we counted them) of the west fork, there's a stand of bracken fern, often waist high, and rock fern that is reminiscent of Hawaii's rain forest. Rock overhangs further down the trail added fantastic touches.

The towering canyon walls of red rock, and granite flanked the idyllic retreat. Crossing the creek at times was slippery business.

There were wet feet, the cool water panacea for tired "dogs" and a part of summer fun.

Our party gasped when a bend in the trail revealed a gathering of bright orange butterflies. Bluejays flitted from tree to tree, keeping a watchful eye, and from a perch in the pines, another bird scolded the hiking party.

A lunch break on a table-top brought more than refreshment. The gurgling creek, the majestic canyon walls, the forest quiet seemed ethereal, relaxing.

Forging ahead, deeper into the forest, we hoped that the ruggedness of the area would prove a natural barrier to hikers without a proper respect for nature.

During our several hours in the canyon, we noted two fishermen casting for trout. Another party used walking sticks to stalk the course of the river, and a couple armed with camera and tripod, overtook us.

The path at times was an obstacle course, with entwining vines and fallen tree trunks to dodge, step over or under.

One hiker reported that the river ahead was captured in a box canyon. Wilson estimated the west fork country at about 20 miles, as it verges into the **Barney Pasture** and **Rogers Lake** area. We estimated we hiked six miles up the river before calling it quits for the day and beginning the long tramp out.

Beauty of West Fork at the bend

THE LAKE LOOP
through lush Northern forests

A lake "loop" in Coconino County's deep forests offers a panacea for heat-tired Valley of the Sun residents in the summer.

Kinnikinick, Ashurst, Mormon and **Lake Mary** are in fairly close togetherness in the Coconino National Forest, south and east of **Flagstaff. Stoneman Lake,** a little apart from the others, can be included for good measure.

The outdoor bonanza offers sun-sparkled lakes, pine-fragrant forest and a chance to fish and camp or just visit. All this plus quiet and relaxation in lush scenery.

Facilities vary from lake to lake. At some, there are established campgrounds with fees. At others, there are no facilities—not even drinking water. Fishing, too, varies, as do boating regulations.

A good prelude to the trip, especially those preparing for overnight stays, is to visit the Coconino National Forest Elden Ranger District office in the Greenlaw shopping center in **Flagstaff.** Personnel provide maps and booklets of interest.

Still another stop for information is the Mormon Lake Ranger Station on the **Lake Mary Road,** out of **Flagstaff.** With current information, visitors can learn about established campgrounds and other facilities. Motorists should have ample supplies of gasoline and water.

At **Ashurst Lake,** some four miles off the main road between **Lake Mary** and **Mormon Lake,** several families were in campers, trailers and tents. At noon, some were fishing from the ease of camp chairs on the lake shore. None bragged about good fishing that day, but the cool breeze was delightful.

Ashurst Dam was constructed in 1954 by the Arizona Game and Fish Department to provide 230 acres of public fishing waters.

Kinnikinick Lake, about 10 gravel road miles from **Mormon Lake,** gets its tongue-twisting name from a shrub that Indians long ago called "Kinnikinic." Several families were camped at the lake. Fishing seemed incidental to the fun of the outing.

Historical **Mormon Lake** received its name when Mormon settlers started a dairy operation at the lake in 1878. It seems that after the settlers left, there were years of deep-snow winters. The spring runoff was heavy. A lake replaced the meadow. Some theorize that the cattle so compacted the meadow soil as to make it a sealant. When the big spring run-off came, the lake was formed.

The largest natural lake in Arizona, according to the forest service,

Summertime fishing at Lake Mary

the 5,000-acre **Mormon Lake** once was a delight for sailing and even supported tour boat operations. But in 1924, the lake began to dry up and today its level fluctuates, leaving extensive marshes exposed.

There are established campgrounds and historic Montezuma Lodge. Mormon Lake Lodge includes a Cowboy Steak House and coffee shop.

The lake swing can be bolstered by adding **Stoneman Lake,** gained by a marked turnoff from Interstate 17. Paving gives way to a gravel road. **Stoneman Lake,** in a pretty setting, is about half privately-owned. There were no public camping facilities in summer 1980.

The lake—some say it is the crater of an old volcano—is named for Gen. George Stoneman (1822-1894). For 15 years, from 1924, there was a post office.

Rustic Mormon Lake Lodge

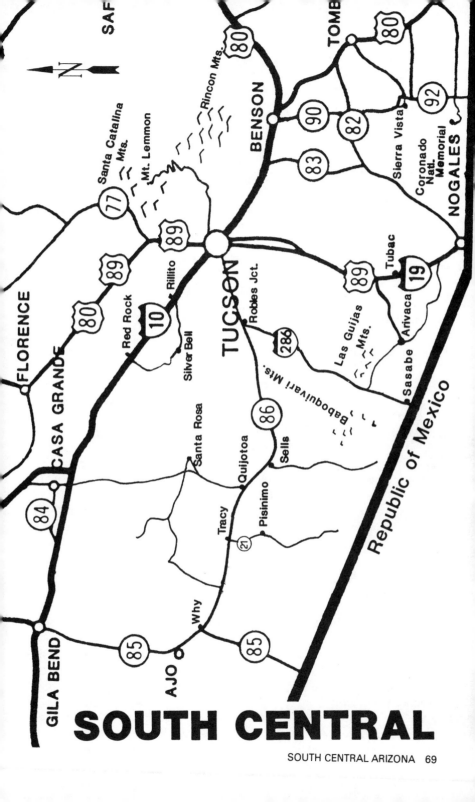

SOUTH CENTRAL

Keeping America beautiful
IN PAPAGO LAND

Four saguaros, each topped with metal crosses, tower at San Jose Mission in **Pisinimo,** while nearby a flock of black crows flits through mesquite and tamarisk trees.

The old church, wrapped in a mantle of quiet dignity, is the big attraction in this remote Papago village.

Although the church's bold portal bespeaks Indian art and culture, the interior is still a pleasant surprise. There, giant abstract murals reflect Papago basketry and pottery motifs.

The Rev. Camillas Kavaganaro, Franciscan missionary at the church during the 1960s when the painting took place, once said the little church reminded him of Psalm 122: "I was glad when they said to me, Let us go into the house of the Lord."

The adobe church, one of dozens in the Papagueria—the land of the Papagos in southern Arizona—was built in 1934 to replace an earlier church.

The striking geometric designs in black, white and red were done by Frank Mariano, a gifted villager. Father Camillas discovered the Papagos' artistry when he noticed Mariano doodling at the trading post. He persuaded him to paint the designs to brighten the old church.

Further enhancing the church one Christmas season, Mariano made a mobile of gourds painted with pottery designs. The mobile still hangs today.

Behind the altar is a mural by David Sine, an Apache artist. It depicts his version of the Lord's Supper.

Near the church is the mission school for about 60 Papago children. On its well-kept playgrounds even trash containers were painted with pottery motifs. One without design carried the inscription: "Indians discovered America—Keep it beautiful."

On a quiet morning, the mission basked beneath smog-free skies. Little Indian girls waved at the advent of visitors.

Adding to the mission compound were the yellow-coated school buildings and home for the Catholic Sisters who teach in the school. A boxcar, also in yellow, serves as the community library.

Pisinimo is 11 miles south of **Arizona 86** between **Why** and **Quijotoa,** on **Indian Route 21.** About 300 Papagos live here, deep in the reservation, an expanse of mountain and desert valley that is bigger than Connecticut.

The people are poor and tend to build their lives around the village and the church. A hub of activity, too, is the Pisinemo Trading Post.

Papago Indian art in church at Pisinimo

(The village name is spelled **Pisinimo** on maps and road signs.)

The James Robinettes, who have owned the trading post 20 years, said their spelling of the name is correct. They said the name means "buffalo head."

The trading post includes a "Basket Room," another colorful surprise brimming with baskets and trays in an assortment of sizes and shapes. All were made by the Papago Indians.

The baskets are made from yucca and beargrass, in natural colors. The black in some designs comes from fibers of the "devil's claw."

The technique used in the baskets is known as coiling. Split stitch baskets are made of beargrass and sewn with yucca so that the coil is exposed to form part of the pattern.

Tiny baskets, one-a-half-inch in diameter, were made of horsehair.

A compact car came bouncing up to the mission and out stepped the Rev. Lambert Fremdling, the shepherd of the church at **Pisinimo.** "Chica," his little dog, was at his heels.

Father Lambert, who has worked on the Papago Reservation 31 years, has been stationed here four years. He also attends missions in six other villages, traveling an average of 3,000 miles a month in the little car.

Papago children trailed Father Lambert on his arrival. When the priest entered his modest quarters, the children were still inquisitive about his guests. They peered through the window, flattening their noses against the pane.

SASABE
life in a small border town!

Capilla de Santa Elena de la Cruz, a tiny mission church, stands on a hill overlooking the remote border town of **Sasabe.** Its white cross contrasts with the blue sky.

Along main street, villagers chat on the porch of the old adobe building. The word "Bar," etched in metal and suspended over the sidewalk, announces the location of El Recreo.

A single car is parked along **Highway 286,** which doubles as Main Street as it winds through town enroute to the port of entry.

The doors of the general store have not yet opened for Saturday's business.

A cold spring wind from **Altar Valley,** nestled along the **Baboquivari Mountains,** blows briskly. Another day has arrived in perhaps the most remote of Arizona's border towns.

The door of one of **Sasabe**'s oldest houses, a well preserved thick-walled adobe, opens and Yvonne Escalante steps outside to pursue another busy day. Mrs. Escalante likes the peace and quiet of the community and its lifestyle.

"Down here, it is an entirely different type life. There isn't the rush, rush, rush. We work hard, but we are just rushing against ourselves. It is a good life. It is quiet and peaceful. If you crave for a little bit of noise, you drive 68 miles to **Tucson,**" she explained.

Until a year ago, her husband, Carlos H. Escalante, and his two sisters had owned the 480-acre town. They had inherited it from their

Port of entry at remote Sasabe

father, Carlos M. Escalante, who came to the site in 1913. He brought his bride to one of the six adobe houses in the settlement in 1924. Later, he acquired the land from his uncle, developed it and named it **Sasabe,** which means "Echo."

Carlos M. Escalante owned all of the buildings, except the church and school, and came to be known as the "Quiet King of Sasabe."

In 1959, while he was still king of all he surveyed, Escalante decided to sell the town. At that time there were 70 residents and 28 buildings. A *Life Magazine* article of March 28, 1970, told of the sale prospect.

But, the sale did not take place during Escalante's lifetime. He died in 1965. The town was sold in March, 1977, to four brothers of Caborca, Sonora.

As a condition of the sale, Carlos H. Escalante kept acreage and a hardware business. He also is engaged in the import of burnt adobe bricks and a mesquite wood business. For relaxation, he fashions clever clocks from native woods—mesquite and ironwood—as well as redwood. The clocks are for sale.

Escalante's sister, Alice Knagge, operates the general store.

Mrs. Escalante helps her husband and works part time in the post office. Her day begins at 5 a.m., when she helps get her two teen-agers ready to board the bus to **Arivaca.** They then will board another bus to Saguarita High School. Riding the bus takes up much of the youngsters' day.

"I wouldn't trade life here for any place. It is a good place to raise small children," Mrs. Escalante said.

The town has a well, electricity and phone service, the latter provided by the Arizona Telephone Co. Subscribers have private lines. Mrs. Escalante sometimes chats via citizens-band radio with her parents in **Arivaca** as her teen-agers prepare to leave for school.

About 30 children, including those from nearby ranches, attend the elementary school. They are taught by a husband-and-wife team, the John Foutys.

Immigration and customs officers and their families live in a compound of more recently-built homes on the outskirts of town. Perhaps 50 persons comprise the population, according to Mrs. Escalante.

Sasabe is reached by taking **State 86** to **Robles Junction,** then traveling south on **State 286.**

Two miles south of the border is **Sasabe, Sonora,** home to about 1,800 persons.

Officials at the port of entry say about 80 persons cross the border during a 16-hour day. Occasionally, they say, some narcotics activity is uncovered.

The little mission church, now no longer used for services, brought a measure of fame to the border town. It was featured in the movie, "Lilies of the Field," starring Sidney Poitier.

OLD ARIVACA
first library, first telegraph

On a March day in 1972, Harvey Riggs, editor of the *Arivaca Briefs,* leaned on a weather-beaten fence rail near an 1880 vintage adobe house and chatted with strangers in the town.

The main street in this homey, peaceful place some 60 miles south of **Tucson,** is flanked by picture-quaint adobe houses, each steeped in a share of history.

"Teresa's Bar was in a corner of the house next door," said Riggs. "Men used to trade a calf for a half-pint whiskey or a horse for a quart."

Old **Arivaca,** sandwiched in a valley between the **San Luis Mountains** and the **Las Guijas,** basks in the bright sunshine. A tavern and grocery store with post office niche mark the remote hub of cattle and ranching operations.

Old trees are in late winter's bleakness. **Arivaca Creek** trickles through the valley and glistens across the roadway beyond.

"**Arivaca** had the first library and the first telegraph in the state," continued editor Riggs. "We were School District No. 2 in Pima County until we consolidated with **Sopori.**

"The government declared **Arivaca** a townsite in 1916 and President Woodrow Wilson signed the deed. Before that, there was a military post here with a detachment of black cavalrymen to take care of the Pancho Villa trouble."

Riggs has been finding things to write about in **Arivaca** territory for 24 years. The excitement that day was a "hippie" wedding up **California Gulch,** and the peaceful quiet of the village had been interrupted with the nuptials trek.

"Cars have been coming through here all day," Riggs said. "I don't know how the word got around."

The latest issue of the breezy, several-page newssheet that is published twice a month, tabbed the climate and spirit of the community as "warm and friendly."

Editor Riggs, in recapping 1971, noted that **Arivaca** had logged five snows and 20 inches of rain, that the new San Ferdinand community church was completed and that the population totaled 120.

In other events chronicled in *"The Briefs,"* Riggs noted that "Terrible Terry is now holding forth in the famous old ghost town of **Ruby,**" and that there was a population explosion down **California Gulch** last spring until forest, health, immigration, customs, state narcotics and Pima and Santa Cruz county sheriffs depopulated the gulch "with the exception of one."

Arivaca's long ago lingers in old adobe walls.

It was reported that the Arizona Game and Fish Department two days before Christmas planted 25,000 four-inch bass; 1,750 three-to-four inch channel catfish and 5,000 bullfrogs in **Arivaca Lake.**

And in a homey note, Rigged penned, "Mary Riggs made and baked about a hundred loaves of bread in 1971."

Arivaca's exact origin seems clouded in old history. **Arivaca,** a Pima Indian word meaning "little reeds" or "little fence water," was abandoned by the Pimas in 1751 during the Pima Revolt. The old Spanish mine nearby, the **San Angeles de Quivavi,** is said to date from 1739.

In another chapter, historians note that the government of Spain in the early 1800s sold about 11,500 acres to Don Ortiz for $747. It was in 1856 that Charles DeVille Poston bought the estate of Arivaca from Tomas and Ignacio Ortiz for $10,000 in gold. A smelter for reducing ore from **Cerro Colorado Mine** (located a few miles away) was established in the mid-19th century.

By April of 1878, there was a post office and businesses in **Arivaca** included two restaurants, a butcher, a blacksmith, brewery, barbershop and six saloons.

OLD TUBAC
and old Tumacacori Mission

The Spanish-aura community of **Tubac,** nestled quietly in the **Santa Cruz Valley,** is a titleholder.

Probably few motorists whizzing along the **Interstate 19 Tucson-Nogales highway** know it is the oldest European settlement in Arizona, dating back almost 250 years.

And **Tubac** claims the first newspaper, *The Arizonian* (established March 3, 1869) and first state park, **The Tubac-Presidio State Park,** 1959. Its first school was established in 1885.

Ruins and contemporary arts meet here. The shops are filled with displays of pottery, jewelry, antiques and woodcarving.

The skyline is dominated by the stark square tower of old St. Ann's Church, built in 1920. The small community stirs visibly on weekends to accommodate curious tourists. Kachina dolls adorn one shop, and craftsmen assemble their wares. A basket maker skillfully weaves bear grass into white and green yucca leaves and devil's claw to create a local specialty.

The village played host to former Presidents Gerald R. Ford and Luis Echeverria Alvarez in important 1974 U.S.-Mexico summit.

It was in this area in 1772 that a 509-man garrison of lancers arrived by order from Spain to establish a post, a presidio. An ancient cannon still guards the door at the museum.

A portion of the old presidio was restored through excavations in 1974 by archeologists from the University of Arizona. It protected a small settlement of miners from Indian raids.

The **Tumacacori Mission,** three miles to the south, was established in 1800 and flourished despite Apache raids throughout the first few decades. In the 1840s, the mission was abandoned and fell into disuse. The first tourists to visit the structure in the early 1850s found it a place of fear and superstition, "except for two or three Germans who did not remain long." It was declared a national monument in 1908.

Today, visitors can venture into the dark, cool interior of the building, shaded by mesquite trees, and walk through the cemetery, **Campo Santo** ("holy field"), to read the legends of the community's forefathers.

St. Anne's Church at Tubac framed by ruins of Tubac Presidio

CORONADO NATIONAL MEMORIAL—view from the top!

Standing at lookout point at **Montezuma Pass** in the **Coronado National Memorial,** a San Diego woman wrote in the visitor book: "So beautiful and close to God."

"Scary" wrote another viewer, and a fearful one noted, "Praying all the way."

Whatever the emotion the trip in this memorial park evokes, the scenery along the gravel road as it coils up from the visitor center to the pass is breathtaking.

The road climbs rapidly, sometimes with sharp horseshoe curves in the **Coronado Forest.** There is a sense of history in the air, as the memorial reflects early Arizona, commemorating the first major exploration into the American southwest by a European.

Coronado National Memorial is about 22 miles south of **Sierra Vista,** and 30 miles west of **Bisbee,** the nearest places for meals and lodging. **Montezuma Canyon Road,** which leads to the memorial, joins **Arizona 92,** about 35 miles west of **Bisbee.** It is five miles from the junction to the memorial headquarters.

There is a picnic area near the visitor center, the latter offering information brochures about the memorial.

Up on **Montezuma Pass viewpoint,** a marker reminds visitors at the spot that in early June, 1540, Coronado's intrepid expedition had progressed down the **San Pedro Valley.**

A breeze sifted through the pass mitigating the July heat. At an altitude of about 6,000 ft., a path wound to the summit of **Coronado Peak.** History and a sense of adventure prompted us to tackle the trail.

Adjusting straw hats to fend off heat and armed with cameras, we felt equal to the half-mile-steep climb. White-wing doves flew over the path and fleecy white clouds etched brilliantly against the blue sky.

Along the way through the yucca, occasional gnarled trees and assorted flora were historical markers, and from time to time there were benches to sit on and contemplate the sights. July is not an ideal time for a climb, but we knew enough to rest and "catch up with our breathing." Although seasoned walkers, we did fail to bring along a canteen of water.

After a while, the trail verged quite steeply. Two teenagers came up full speed, emphasizing what we already knew—age does make a difference. A man and his wife stopped to chat and tell us about an interesting ghost town in southern Arizona. There is something about the outdoors that breds easy sociability.

Resting place atop Coronado Peak Trail

Once at the top, we had the summit to enjoy by ourselves. The only exception to the complete solitude was a colony of bright orange ladybugs clinging to the trunk of a dead tree.

The view from the pinnacle overlooking the vast expanses—some in Arizona—some in Mexico—offered purple shadowed mountains, and colorful desert. Somehow, it reminded of the age-old hymn—"This Is My Father's World."

It was a mountain top experience. It was good to have been there.

SILVER BELL
—the mine and the town.
Say it with a tinkle!

Silver Bell's past and present rests in the copper gouged from the earth—but its name, **Silver Bell,** brings to mind the tingling lilt of yuletide.

A Christmas stamp issued in 1965 helped put the community on the map.

But, **Silver Bell** was named for the old **Silver Bell Mine** and the old mining camp of **Silverbell** (it was one word in those days) that has since vanished from the face of the rugged hill country about four miles northwest.

Origin of the first **Silverbell** name is clouded. But there are tales. Some say it was named for a desert flower. Others that it was named for a dance hall proprietor named Bell, whose hair was prematurely gray.

Still another version is that Spaniards found a chunk of silver here big enough to fashion a bell.

Except for the mining that gave birth to both the old and the new towns, any resemblance between the two must be coincidental. The old Silverbell was marked with saloons, murders and shoot "em-ups." A historian referred to the old town as a "hell hole."

Don Jameson, general superintendent of the American Smelting and Refining company's (ASARCO) **Silver Bell Mine,** said a Tucson doctor once kept on his desk a bottle half full of bullets taken from old **Silverbell's** residents.

But **Silver Bell**—today—is much different.

At high noon a soft breeze sweeps down the saddle between the **Silverbell** and **Waterman Mountains.** The background drone comes from trucks rushing ore from the huge open pit mine to the mill in this town about 22 miles west of the **Silver Bell** turnoff from **Interstate 10.**

A peaceful quietness and slower pace pervades as spring bursts forth. On a Saturday morning, patrons drop in at the little third-class post office, then linger outside in the warm sunshine to chat with friends.

Tall eucalyptus trees mark a residential street. Children pedal their bikes, dogs scamper about. This company-owned town, founded in 1951 by ASARCO, is home for 225 families. Houses are look-alikes. There's a grocery market, service station, barber and beauty shop.

A company-provided building houses the community hall where special quarters are shared by the Catholic and Federated (Protest-

Old ore cart at Silver Bell

ant) churches.

Silver Bell claimed the national spotlight in 1965 when it was the "first-day cover" town for the red, green and yellow Christmas postage stamp. There were 705,000 first day cancellations in the unexpected deluge. Extra workers in the Tucson Post Office assisted. And folks all over the country bundled up their Christmas cards and sent them to be remailed with the Christmasy-sounding postmark.

School children here are bussed to **Marana,** and many towns-people are boosters for the Marana High School team.

"Everybody does their own thing here," one resident observed. Bridge, softball, bowling in **Tucson,** and a summertime youth recreation program directed by the Pima County Recreation Department are among other activities.

Big event every year is the company barbecue on Labor Day.

Jameson pointed out that the new **Silver Bell Mine** was the first open-pit operation in the **Tucson** area. Others now are larger.

"We mill about 11,000 tons of ore daily," he said. "The pit covers the area of four other old mines, including the **Mammoth** and **Imperial.** To this day we still run across old machinery."

There are other old mines in the area, some nearby, but the **Silver Bell** is the only mine in operation.

Ore was discovered in the area as early as the 1860s. Historians note that the **Mammoth** and **Old Boot** mines were taken over by the Imperial Copper Co. in 1902. A smelter was built at **Sasco,** eight miles from the mine, and in a major event, the Arizona-Southern Railroad was built from **Red Rock** to **Silverbell** in 1904.

In the next several years, the camp was said to have produced about $1 million in metal annually. Population boomed and so did lawlessness.

Disaster struck when mine owners developed financial trouble in **Tombstone** mines and were forced into bankruptcy, dragging down the sibsidiary Imperial Copper Co.

Later, other firms took over the operation successfully until a drop in copper prices halted activities in about 1921. It is said that in the banner year 1917 that copper valued at $2,124,000 was produced in the mine.

Total demise came in 1934 when the railroad was ripped out and the Sasco smelter dismantled.

Today's **Silver Bell** was founded in 1951. In December, 1981, an *Arizona Republic* story stated that the **Silver Bell Copper Mine** "is being closed until the copper market improves."

MT. LEMMON
Tucson's mountain retreat

An oasis in the desert, the **Mt. Lemmon Recreation Area** in the **Santa Catalina Mountains** combines vacation travel with welcome relief from the heat in the summertime.

The drive from the **Tanque Verde Road,** northeast of **Tucson,** yields a kaleidoscope of scenery with rapid transition in weather and plant life. At the crest, 9,196 feet in elevation, the weather on a summer day is cool and crisp.

There is an extra bonus for motorists with four-wheel drive vehicles or hikers willing to walk down a jeep trail, which juts off near the U.S. Air Force Radar Station.

Along this trail, lacy ferns grow lushly, sometimes several feet tall. Other notes are flowers in a rainbow of colors, Arizona pines and conifers, huddles of quaking white-stemmed aspens and tiny green meadows.

The **Catalinas** form a lofty backdrop for **Tucson.** Highest is **Mt. Lemmon,** focal point of a 38,000-acre recreation area. The 30-mile **Hitchcock Highway** up through the **Catalinas** to the summit was named for a former publisher who advocated the road so that the wonderland would be more accessible to the public. The road, begun in 1933, was completed in 1950.

The diversified scenery is predicated on the rising altitude. A Forest Service marker at **Windy Point Vista** describes the changing vegetation at various altitudes. The vista point, one of several, overlooks **Tucson** and faraway mountains and valleys.

Giant saguaros and other Sonoran desert flora mark the area to about the 4,000-foot level. Then follow the semi-arid grasslands, sycamores, cottonwoods and willows of **Molino Canyon,** blue oaks, pinons and manzanitas.

The panorama moves to **Cathedral Rock,** Arizona cypress, **Bear Canyon,** chaparral, scrub oak, and rock formations that can be interpreted in design as imaginative as the viewer.

In the forest zone, beginning around 7,000 feet, conifers and Arizona pines scent the air, and every turn in the road is picture pretty. The skyland playground is marked with picnic sites. One trail leads to a fire lookout tower on **Mt. Bigelow.**

Seeking the area for relief from the heat is nothing new. Soldiers stationed at **Ft. Lowell** near **Tucson** in the 1880s had the same idea. They rode horses to reach the area.

The weather at the top has been likened to Southern Canada.

Vista of canyons and mountains

Reportedly, in a trip to the top from **Tucson,** one passes through all the climatic zones met on a 1,500-mile trip to the northland.

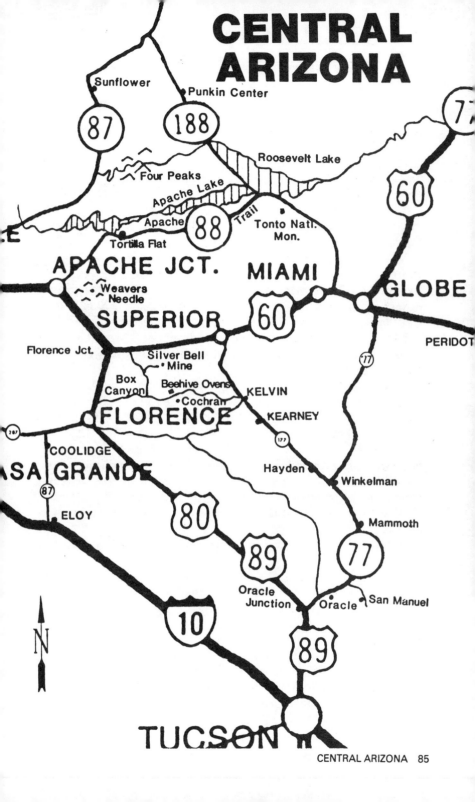

CENTRAL ARIZONA

Sunflower
Punkin Center
87
188
77
Roosevelt Lake
60
Four Peaks
Apache Lake
Apache 88 Trail
Tonto Natl. Mon.
Tortilla Flat
APACHE JCT.
MIAMI
GLOBE
Weavers Needle
SUPERIOR
60
PERIDOT
Florence Jct.
Silver Bell Mine
77
Box Canyon
Beehive Ovens
KELVIN
Cochran
KEARNEY
FLORENCE
177
COOLIDGE
Hayden
Winkelman
ASA GRANDE
207
87
80
Mammoth
ELOY
89
77
Oracle Junction
Oracle
San Manuel
10
89
N
TUCSON

TRAIL TO FOUR PEAKS
and down to Punkin Center

The early morning sun had just risen as four sleepy-eyed passengers got into the four-wheel drive vehicle for a jostling trip to **Four Peaks** in the **Mazatzal Mountains.**

It was a maiden voyage for the 1968 Jeep Wagoneer as far as the new owners were concerned, and the rugged road was chosen to test the merits of the vehicle.

The rough part began as the jeep left **Beeline Highway,** about 13.5 miles from **Shea Boulevard** and half-mile past the first viewpoint. A log of mileage and scenery was kept to record the journey.

Mile 0.0—Veering right, the dirt road (not noted on the map) wound through the desert, marked with saguaro cacti and palo verde trees. "Wow," commented a rider as **Four Peaks** loomed in the distance. "Are we really going to the top of the peaks?" Actually, the trail was going into the timberline below the bleak part of the peaks.

Mile 3.2—The road forks. We turned right on Forest Road 143.

Mile 4—At a covered feed trough and a corral with two cows, we pulled over. Six cars passed.

Mile 4.3—A Forest Service sign warned, "Narrow hazardous mountain road, unsafe for public travel." The road certainly was not for dudes. With the four-wheel drive and experienced drivers, we decided to push on.

Mile 4.6—A sign, "Mine Mountain Springs." The scenery changed, featuring odd rock formations and a forest of cacti. Quail scooted through the underbrush. The road coiled upward, widening in some areas, narrow and "washboardy" in others.

Mile 8—A car lay in the ravine below, a mute reminder to be careful.

Mile 10.3—**Fisher Springs.** Dense desert growth. The changing vegetation was amazing.

Mile 10.6—A trickle of water glistened in the sun as **Picadilla Creek** snaked across the road. More quail.

Mile 10.9—A wide area devasted by fire. New growth coming up through the old burn and skeletons of old trees. A roadrunner made a mad dash up the road.

Mile 11.7—Cline's Cabin just off the road, and a sign gave notice of **Mud Springs** and **Soldier Camp Trail.** Several cars on the road. Little blue and yellow flowers were unexpected mid-November sights.

Mile 14.2—Another creek bed. Trees in autumn dress canopied the stream, with a vista of **Four Peaks** in the background. Two cars full of Boy Scouts wheeled by.

Four Peaks loom majestically in distance.

Mile 15—**Tehanus Spring,** where someone had lighted a campfire. Nearing the base of the peaks, the road, sometimes with edges washed out, grew very rugged, pitching and rocking us inside the jeep.

Mile 18.8—The crest of the main trail, elevation about 5,700 feet, and a right turn on a ragged road to the peaks. On one side, a lake nestled in the distant mountains. On the other side, **Roosevelt Lake** and **Tonto Basin** were all but obliterated by a pall of smog.

Mile 18.9—A sign: "Entering Three Bar Wildlife Area, Tonto National Forest, maintained for Game, Watershed and Range Research." Then, into the deep forest.

Mile 19.6—**Pigeon Springs,** picnic tables, trickling spring, fireplace. Great. Explored around, talked to a couple of hunters. Eying the climb out, we switched to four-wheel drive and were satisfied at the vehicle's pulling power on the steep, rutted trail. Back on the rim road, there were pleasant picnic sites tucked beneath gnarled old trees.

Mile 20.6—The end of the road. Two deer spotted. Interesting place to explore. We lamented again the smog that ruined the view below of the lake and **Tonto Basin.**

Mile 21.3—Back off the side road, over a cattle guard crossing and a right turn to begin the descent on the **Tonto Basin** side on the **El Oso Road.**

Mile 23.7—Time to picnic in the bright, warm sunshine. Picnic fare and hot coffee delicious in the mountain air. Not a car passed. Resumed travel. Rugged descent a real experience.

Mile 31.5—The road joined **Arizona 188,** offering three choices for the return route: **Punkin Center** and **Payson Highway; Roosevelt Lake** and the **Apache Trail,** or **Globe** and **Superior.** We chose the former and shortest route.

Taking a short cut beyond **Punkin Center** for the **Payson Highway,** we hit the paved highway at a total dirt road mileage of 49.9

It had been a good day to remember.

Trail out of Pigeon Springs picnic area

Theodore Roosevelt Dam—built in 1911.

APACHE TRAIL
Tortilla Flat to Tonto ruins

The sign says "**Tortilla Flat,** the biggest little town in Arizona. Population 5."

The buildings look rustic, inviting. So, travelers naturally bail out for a closer look.

Tortilla-shaped rocks gave the name to the town that long ago served as a rest stop for high-wheeled wagons, mule teams and men hauling supplies to **Roosevelt Dam.**

Inside the store and restaurant there is music, curios, a variety of books and friendly people.

The novel place is only one of the landmarks along the **Apache Trail,** a desert scenic treat not far from **Phoenix.**

Early in the morning, four travelers in one party had stashed ample picnic and camera supplies in the car and headed for the hills. Years had passed since they tackled the route with its rugged **Fish Creek Hill.** The trail plus the return through **Miami** is now an easy, fun one-day junket.

Turning off **U.S. 60** at **Apache Junction** and on to **State 88,** the

Superstition Mountains loom purple and mysterious—silhouetted against the rising sun.

Meandering down the trail, **Canyon Lake** vista point is soon at hand.

The lake glistens in the sun and boaters are already plying the waters. Picnic ramadas are filling, and other boats are still moored at the marina.

Near the top of **Fish Creek Hill** is a deep-lined gorge and a chance to take a cautious look.

The road widens after **Fish Creek** bridge. In a short time, **Apache Lake,** nestled against the mesquite and greasewood dotted hills, bursts on the horizon.

Apache Lake meanders along to **Roosevelt Dam,** at times paralleling and adding extra interest to the trail. **Roosevelt Dam** is billed as the largest masonry dam in the world. President Teddy Roosevelt was on hand for its dedication in 1911.

Tonto National Monument, with cliff dwellings occupied by Salado Indians 600 years ago, is about three miles from **Roosevelt.**

There is a sense of achievement on reaching the cliff dwellings and resting in the cool shade. But, for us, there is one dismaying note.

Only one exposure remains in the camera. Other film is in the car —far below in the parking lot.

Tortilla Flat—"biggest little town in Arizona" on the Apache Trail

BOX CANYON
and a rough, rutted road

Travel in an awesome box canyon in the mountains northeast of **Florence** has its scenic rewards, but it is a white-knuckle, four-wheel drive vehicle trip definitely not for the faint-hearted.

Travelers should beware that the road is rough and dangerous.

Our group of four in a four-wheel drive Jeep Wagoneer stalled out in a wash. At another point, the road was so bad that it had to be built up before we could pass over it.

We also discovered an overturned Toyota Landcruiser on a side-road beyond the canyon. Its driver miscalculated the grade of the rutted road.

The trip, however, is a challenge, and it blends desert beauty with a real sense of adventure.

Our concern was whether our long-wheelbase four-wheeler could maneuver the trail without smashing some underpinning or possibly rupturing the gas tank.

Actually, the day was saved when two obliging young men we met on the road built up the dangerous spot, then directed us across the hazard.

We had not expected the going to be so rough. Twelve years ago we made the trip in a passenger car. Today the trail through the box canyon is different. Devasting storms, rains, floods and time have taken their toll.

The rock canyon walls are spectacular, and the desert is picture-postcard pretty. In places, the mountains appear as pin cushions for hundreds of saguaro cacti.

Coveys of quail dashed across the road or clustered in the shade of palo verde and mesquite trees. There were rabbits, doves, squirrels and even roadrunners.

At the start, the road, which parallels a railroad track off of **U.S. 80,** is dusty, full of dips and washes. It winds by ranches, then veers north near the site of the Ashurst-Hayden Dam.

Sometimes the road faded away through washes, but could be picked up beyond. When our vehicle stalled in a wash, we had to switch to four-wheel drive. Already, it was obvious that the trek should not be made in rainy weather or even if the rain threatens.

We were watching the road like hawks when the first really bad stretch loomed. It looked as if our trip through the canyon was over, but we decided to hike ahead to check things out. It was heartening to see a smaller four-wheel drive vehicle ahead of us.

The owners, two young men with special equipment, were practic-

Nosing around the curve in Box Canyon

ing mountain climbing but interrupted their activity to come to our rescue.

We continued through the canyon, but even then we were not out of danger. Time after time, John Lynch bailed out of the car to serve as guide, signalling to my husband, Don, where to steer the car through the rocks and ruts.

Finally, we topped out of the canyon where the desert was a color medley of mesquite, cacti, mountains and blue sky.

At a "Y" in the road, we headed for the old **Silver Bell** mine camp area in another canyon. The road, boasting two old windmills, was divided at various points and was sometimes narrow and eroded. We chose the trail that appeared more travelled and in better shape.

The **Silver Bell** property, including a shaded glen area of **Martinez Canyon,** was posted *"Keep Out."*

However, Peter Villaverde, Jr., former state legislator and an overseer for the property, graciously gave us permission to visit.

Villaverde said the mine property, more than 100 years old, is owned by the California Steel Products Co.

The property, private patented land in the Pioneer Mining District, includes the site of an old bar, house and mines beyond.

Martinez Canyon, flanked with salmon-color rock cliffs, provided a pretty setting for a tailgate picnic.

It was on the road to **Superior Highway** where we happened onto the overturned Toyota. The vehicle had flipped on its side in the middle of a rough, steep road covered with loose rocks and soil.

From the location and steepness of the grade, it appeared that the owners had their work cut out for them if they tried to get the Toyota back on its wheels again.

The sight was a sobering reminder that four-wheeling can be dangerous.

Vehicle that didn't make it

TORTUOUS TRAIL
TO THE BEEHIVE OVENS

Our party of four knew we were in for a rugged trip.

We had purposely chosen a four-wheel drive vehicle route to the old "beehive" ovens on a secluded mountainside overlooking the Gila River, some 30 miles east of Florence.

We wanted adventure, but not in the measure that developed.

John and Winifred Lynch, my husband Don and I followed a three-year-old plan, complete with mileage between check points and instructions to take the correct forks in the road.

The venture began with a turn to the right off the highway to **Globe,** about four miles east of **Florence Junction.**

The road criss-crossed and followed desert washes, past a crumbling cabin, old wells, mine-pocked hills. There were quaint windmills, curious cattle and an old corral of ocotillo limbs. Not knowing what lay ahead, several leisurely stops were made.

The road got rougher, but we were still on target. Visions of charcoal-broiled steaks began to surface.

About 19 miles inland from the highway turnoff, the car was shifted into four-wheel drive for improved maneuvering ability. The car growled and groaned up a ridge, only to face an even worse descent.

Lynch bailed out to walk ahead, directing the driver to veer the car left or right to miss high centers, and to avoid boulders or drops in the road. The three-tenths mile distance from the ridge to the wash seemed an eternity.

There was more of the same ahead. And worse. Mrs. Lynch and I got out of the car and walked up the hill. At times, Lynch added rocks to build up the trail. The wildly beautiful scenery was ignored.

It was Mrs. Lynch's opinion that the "road" must be the worst in the U.S.A. Heatwole said he would never attempt the trail again except in case of "life or death."

At a turn to the right to reach the ovens, the trail became faint, hardly discernible and even worse to negotiate. Driving became tense and Mrs. Lynch and I, who had kept up a running patter, got the impression the men preferred silence. For a time we walked ahead of the crawling car.

Actually, the vehicle deserved an "A-plus" for performance. We simply had not envisioned the trail conditions nor the time involved. It was 3 p.m. when we reached the ovens overlooking the Gila in the distance.

An oldtimer has said the oven structures were smelters in which

Ancient charcoal smelters—lures for the traveler

charcoal was burned. The open holes were for hooks which held the ore buckets. The ovens reportedly were built in the 1850's by a group of miners from Scotland.

The ovens are of native stone and about 30 ft. high. Each has a doorway at the bottom, with opening in the back top of the oven. One had been converted into living quarters, complete with sink and stove. Small cacti grew on top another oven. The structures were well preserved, probably because of their inaccessibility.

At the ovens we received dismaying news. Desert survival class members who had waded the Gila to reach the ovens said they would not cross the river in their four-wheel drive vehicles nor tackle the road up from the river.

Apparently, we would have to retrace much of the tortuous road. It was too late in the day. We would never make it before dark. While assessing our food supply for an overnight stay and wondering if relatives at home would note our absence, we heard two four wheel drive vehicles rumbling up the road this side of the river.

Way to the ovens is plenty rough

The young drivers informed us that it was possible to cross the Gila at a particular point, reached by another tortuous trail in the mountains.

The Gila was rushing by as we paused before nosing our car into the stream. Quicksand could be a problem. Lynch waded cautiously ahead to determine the right path and gave the okay. The car balked at first in pulling out at the bank, and it was comforting to note the two young couples in their four wheel drive vehicles crossing the river behind us.

The sun was setting and casting long shadows from giant tamarisk trees as we crossed the railroad track and jostled up to nearby buildings, part of ghost town **Cochran.** There was just time for a quick look around the old buildings.

We were not completely "out of the woods" until we hit the well-traveled road and turned right to **Florence.**

It had been a day to remember. And to experience through the comfort of armchair reading.

In 1981, we attempted to reach the ovens by turning off the **Riverside-Florence Road** to cross the Gila River in the vicinity of old **Cochran.** The river was running full and deep with no possible chance of crossing it. At one point along the rough dirt road in to the river, about five miles from the **Riverside-Florence** turnoff intersection, an open mine shaft gaped dangerously some 30 feet from the road. *VISITORS MUST BEWARE OF MINES!* The former mining camp and railroad station at **Cochran** had been obliterated.

(Arizona Republic files note that the ovens were at a mining town called **Butte.** The townsite was laid out by a Pinal Consolidated mining official, and the place once boasted a Chinese restaurant, store, boarding houses and a telephone line. The post office, established in 1883, was discontinued in 1886.)

Studying the terrain before nosing jeep into river

SCENIC SWING
thru Pinal mining towns

Oracle, Winkelman, Kelvin, Kearney, Hayden, Mammoth, San Manuel.

If these Arizona places sound unfamiliar, then a loop through eye-popping desert scenery can offer a fun opportunity to learn more about the state's variety and vastness.

Throw in a look at Kennecott Copper Corporation's **Ray** copper pit, one of the country's largest; inspect an old compressed-air locomotive that once moved men and supplies in an underground mine, now ensconced in **Kearney;** marvel at towering smoke stacks—and the insight grows.

The paved route of about 250 miles (depending on extra side trips) can be easily traveled in one day. Take along a picnic lunch and state map.

Start early, preferably before dawn and watch daybreak as you travel east on **State Route 60.** Breakfast enroute, perhaps at **Apache Junction.**

At **Superior,** turn on **State Route 177** to **Kearney** and **Winkelman.** Meantime, keep an eye out for the "Welcome" sign and a viewpoint turnoff to the Ray Copper open pit. The scene is awesome.

A short distance away on the highway, the curious may take a side trip (about 2.5 miles) to the small communities of **Kelvin** and **Riverside** which are separated by the **Gila River.**

A store sits on the site of the old **Riverside** stage stop. **Kelvin** was named for Kelvin Grove in Scotland and had its origin in early mining days.

Back on the main highway, **State Route 177,** the next destination is **Kearney,** a relatively new town, founded in 1958. It was constructed by Kennecott to house mine workers and families.

The town was named for Stephen Watts Kearney, a major in the U.S. Army. The locomotive monument prompts reflection on old mining activities.

Pushing on, a sign along the highway, "Welcome to Kennecott Country," anounces the next town on the loop, **Hayden.**

Hayden was named for Charles Hayden of the company which operates mines near the community. The post office was established here in 1910.

Winkelman, the next stop, is a trade center for surrounding mines and stock ranches. Oddly, a cemetery reposes in the middle of the town.

Enshrined locomotive at Kearney

Leaving **Winkelman,** and going south on **State Route 177,** the next 20-mi. travel lap, paralleling the **San Pedro River** to **Mammoth,** offers a relaxing interlude. **Mammoth,** once a lusty mining town, is now quiet, and travelers must detour off the highway to the town's older "main" street. The Mammoth Mine was worked as early as 1873.

Towering smoke stacks appear during the approach to **San Manuel.** A turnoff from **State 77** to **State Route 76,** about five miles from **Mammoth,** leads to **San Manuel,** a Magma Copper Co. town that was established in 1953 to recover copper deposits.

After returning to **State Route 77,** travelers must again dip slightly off the highway for a swing into **Oracle.** Before browsing through the vintage town, picnic in a nearby wooded area.

Historic sights in **Oracle** include the Old Mountain View Hotel, built in 1895 and now a part of the Baptist church. Buffalo Bill Cody was a visitor at the hotel off and on between 1910 and 1916.

Another **Oracle** claim to fame is that novelist Harold Bell Wright reportedly stayed at Rancho Linda Vista during the time he wrote *The Mine with the Iron Door.*

Oracle Historical Society members provide community information at their Acadia Ranch Museum. The museum is operated by volunteers 2 to 6 p.m., Wednesday through Saturday.

A museum door with mail drop reminds of the days when the ranch contained the town's first post office in 1882.

A sign on the door tells of other building activities—a morgue, a TB sanitarium, and a friendly ghost named George. Tom Thompson, society president, said there probably was no sanitarium but "lungers" were among the boarders.

Agnes Ramsay, widow of Reginald Ramsay who bought the ranch in 1943, said they were told about the ghost at the time.

The historical society, with about 150 members, is purchasing the property for the museum.

"The place in many ways had been a center of town," Thompson said. "It had the first post office, the first telephone and first television."

Oracle was named for the ship which Albert Weldon, one of the early pioneers, took around "The Horn" on his way to the area.

The **Pinal Pioneer Parkway** (U.S. Route 80) begins the return route. Signs along the parkway point out the various desert flora. Roadrunners may put in an appearance.

Motorists are attracted to a memorial for movie star Tom Mix, "whose spirit left his body at this exact spot" in a 1940 traffic accident.

To get back to **Phoenix,** take **State Route 287,** then **State 387,** to **Interstate 10.**

PERIDOT
and the rich, green gemstone

A small mission church, built in 1893 to serve as a place of worship for 400 San Carlos Apache Indians, sits on a hill overlooking the community of **Peridot.** Behind it looms the **Peridot Mesa.**

Up in the mesa's recesses, men, women and children hack at the volcanic rocks in search of rich deposits of a green gemstone—the peridot.

Elsewhere, down the road from the old church, the Peridot Trading Post already is bustling. Another day of gemstone mining has started in this reservation community southeast of Globe.

The mesa is a major source of the peridot stone, which ranges in hue from vibrant yellow-green to a rich deep green. Other sources include an island in the Red Sea, Africa and Burma.

A report at the **Arizona Mineral Museum** estimates that the **Peridot Mesa** contains approximately four square miles in which minable quantities of peridot can be found.

San Carlos tribesmen extract peridot-bearing rocks from 10 to 15 shallow pits cut into the basalt lava that covers the top of the large mesa.

An ancient belief once held that the peridot, when powdered, was a remedy for asthma. People today, however, prize the gemstone, formed originally in the fires of a volcano, for its beauty.

Mission church and school at Peridot

Peridot stones featured in ring and bolo tie

Melvin Montgomery's trading post at **Peridot** contains an assortment of polished gemstones mounted in gold-color jewelry. Rough peridot stones also are sold there. The Peridot Enterprise shop, owned by the San Carlos Apache Tribe, is on **U.S. Highway 70,** at **Cutter.**

Montgomery said the stones may be mined only by residents of the reservation and added that a tribe ordinance forbids outsiders from going to the mesa. It seems that in the past non-Indians brought machinery to the mesa to strip out the peridots.

"Why shouldn't the Indians protect their property?" he asked.

Permits to visit the mesa can be obtained from the tribal office or the Tribal Tourism Department in **San Carlos.**

Ned Anderson, tribal chairman, said permits are issued only after an applicant's proposal has been deemed suitable. He confirmed that only those living on the reservation are allowed to dig for the gemstones.

Back at the Lutheran-mission compound, the Rev. Dennis Meier was preparing for Sunday services. About half the members would show up, he predicted.

The old church is a source of many stories—including one about the long flight of stairs leading to the structure.

Years ago, a truck loaded with cement halted at the church and the driver announced that if forms for church steps could be made right away, he would provide the concrete.

Members got in high gear to take advantage of the generous offer.

NORTHEAST ARIZONA

NEW MEXICO

UTAH

ARIZONA

40

Canyon De Chelly Natl. Mon.

63

Ganado

Monument Valley

CHINLE

KAYENTA

Second Mesa

TSEGI

Cow Springs

Rainbow Bridge Natl. Mon.

Navajo Natl. Mon.

Betatakin

Elephant Feet

87

98

Tonalea

160

264

PAGE

Tuba City

Cameron

FLAGSTAFF

89

89

66

89A

89A

WILLIAMS

N

RAINBOW BRIDGE
and canyons of Lake Powell

A rainbow, carved in stone, towers majestically at the end of one of **Lake Powell's** remote canyon recesses.

The bridge area is reached by a boat trip starred with panoramic sandstone cliffs in mind-boggling shapes, sizes and tapestry effects. And **Rainbow Bridge,** wrought by water and the elements through the eons, engenders its own pot of gold in awe.

A visitor from Iowa, writing in the registry near the foot of the bridge, noted: "Eighth Wonder of the World."

A tiny plaque speaks of another dimension: "Those who pause to rest within the shadow of the bridge will leave their troubles behind."

Passengers, boarding an excursion cruiser at **Wahweap Marina,** had rounded a bend in **Bridge Canyon** waters. They gasped at their first glimpse of the salmon-shade span arched against the sky. Some 290 feet in height, it is the world's largest natural arch.

The fascinating sight just inside Utah is reached from Arizona waters. Passengers lost no time disembarking to hike the quarter-mile watch-your-step path to the bridge.

Earlier, passengers had boarded a glass-enclosed boat, and enroute the pilot had pointed out such landmarks as Castle Rock, Gunsight Butte, Needle and Crown points, Last Chance and Cathedral canyons. There are about 91 major canyons needling from the lake.

Along the way, passengers sipped coffee, tea, soft drinks and watched the mountain and lake panorama. After a rest stop at **Rainbow Bridge Marina,** there were sack lunches. Then came the breathtaking view of **Rainbow Bridge.**

Many famous people have visited the bridge, including Theodore Roosevelt and author Zane Gray in 1913. President Taft set aside the bridge as a national monument in 1910.

Photographers on our tour had a heyday, and ample time was allowed for the hike to the rainbow arch.

Rainbow Bridge was a hard act to follow, but surprisingly, the next travel milestone, a cruise through **Forbidden Canyon,** was not anti-climactic.

Magnificent huge sandstone cliffs towered on all sides. Some were streaked naturally with "Desert Varnish," creating a tapestry effect. In **Friendship Cove,** the boat navigated narrow channels, once with another boat not far away.

During the trip, both pilot and co-pilot gave out an educational patter, pointing out novel formations, depth of the lake, its history.

Until the formation of **Lake Powell** in the mid 1960s, **Rainbow**

Bridge was reached by a long, grueling hike. Now it's an easy one-day trip from **Wahweap.**

Actually, it would take days to see highlights of the lake and its major canyons. The one-day trip whets the appetite for more of the lake story.

Motor travel to **Page** and **Wahweap** from the **Phoenix** area offers an interesting and changing panorama of Arizona scenery.

Approach to awesome Rainbow Bridge   (Northeast Arizona) RAINBOW BRIDGE **105**

MONUMENT VALLEY
panorama of color

Even from a distance they beckon—the tall spires, the pinnacles in fantasy shapes—all promising more wonders to come.

Monument Valley, considered one of the "Seven Wonders of Navajo Land," straddles the Arizona-Utah border. It offers a panorama of scapes in magentas, mauves, burnt reds dusted with purples.

Before venturing into the Monument Valley Navajo Tribal Park, our party of four spent the night at the famed Goulding's Lodge. As we watched from the motel porch, the monuments changed hues and shadows as the afternoon and evening progressed.

This historic lodge is built on a rock bench above the valley floor with a giant brick-red monolith soaring hundreds of feet behind.

Promptly at 6:30 p.m., a quaint bell sounded and reverberated against the vermillion cliffs. It was the single hour for the family-style dinner. Guests converged on the dining hall where salads, big bowls of mashed potatoes, peas, cottage cheese and platters of sliced ham and homemade bread graced the tables.

Later there was a color slide program at the lodge.

Next morning, we boarded a four-wheel drive, air-conditioned vehicle for a three-hour tour of the valley. The trail was marked "Travel at your own risk." We were glad to leave the driving to Silas Cly, our Indian driver. Cost of the tour was $12 per person, in 1974.

The men in our party and Silas came to the rescue of an Illinois couple whose compact car was stuck in the sand.

Motorists scarcely noticed the bouncing, jostling ride, at times, through powder-fine red dust. Nature's creations in such shapes as The Mittens, Big Chief, Setting Hen, Stage Coach and Bear Eating Honey, to name a few, were fascinating.

At **Echo Cave,** with dwellings 800 to 1200 years old, a well-placed echo would reverberate eight times. A stop at a hogan revealed an Indian mother, colorfully attired in bright red blouse and turquoise jewelry, weaving at her loom.

Indians, who still live and tend their sheep in the isolation of this valley, add to the interest of the visit.

ARIZONA INDIAN COUNTRY
wind-swept Navajo lands, Hopi mesas

A trip through the sculptured sandstone scenery of Navajo land, combined with a visit to Hopi Mesa country, can provide a truly unusual vacation.

The opportunity to inspect ancient relic-land splashed with color combines pleasingly with a sense of solitude that dominates this remote land in northeastern Arizona.

On a three-day swing into the reservation country, we confined driving to paved roads, finding comfortable lodging at **Monument Valley, Chinle** and **Second Mesa.**

A turn off **U.S. Highway 89** north of **Cameron** onto **U.S. 160** points the traveler toward **Tuba City.** We made a brief detour to examine dinosaur footprints left in rocks from a prehistoric age.

More interesting than the prints, however, were the small improvised tepees nearby where Navajo women and girls sold handmade bead necklaces.

Along Main Street in **Tuba City,** a modern hospital and the new housing contrasted with older sandstone buildings.

Elephant Feet, giant stone monoliths familiar from picture postcards, were a landscape surprise as we continued north toward **Tonalea.**

Travelers should carry ample supplies when traveling in the northland. Commercial eating places are scarce.

Navajo National Monument is reached by taking **Navajo 564** southwest of **Kayenta** between **Cow Springs** and **Tsegi.** The scenic drive through juniper country proved a good side junket.

After enjoying the picnic facilities at the monument, we tackled the **Sandal Trail** for a vista of ruins of **Betatakin.** The ruins were built by the Anasazi Indians whose culture flourished in the 1200s. **Sandal Trail** is a half-mile nature trail where a sign reminds you, "Safety is your own responsibility," as you wind through yucca, Mormon tea plants and buffalo berry bushes.

The monument headquarters building, at an altitude of 6,286 feet, offers a slide presentation of the area, plus display of arts and crafts.

Three great cliff dwellings mark the culmination of the Anasazi culture in the **Kayenta** area. By about 1300, the Anasazi had abandoned their homes and fields. The **Kayenta** district is now inhabited by Navajos who have been there about 100 years and are not related to the prehistoric Anasazi.

A tour of **Monument Valley,** straddling the Arizona-Utah line, is a **must** on the **Navajo Trail** swing. Another interesting and beautiful

Betatakin Lookout Point

place to visit is **Canyon de Chelly,** near **Chinle,** with its beautiful steep walls and ruins of prehistoric Indian dwellings.

The Hubbell Trading Post and the museum at **Ganado** are well worth a stop. The trading post, founded in 1878, is still a hub of trading activity for the Navajos and offers everything from groceries to rugs in an early-day setting of wooden-beamed ceilings hung with horse collars and lanterns.

Our last stop was at the Hopi Cultural Center and Museum on the wind-swept **Second Mesa.** The pueblo-style building includes a motel, museum, arts display and restaurant.

At dinner time, little Hopi "Headstarters" from nearby **Oraibi** delighted guests with a dance performance.

Later that night, the smell of a campfire and the beating of drums and chanting from a 49'ers-sponsored dance provided a fitting finale to a visit to the land of the "Peaceful People," as the Hopis are called.

CANYON DE CHELLY
the canyon of surprises

Cottonwood and willow tree leaves shimmied in a breeze as the ponderous 6-wheel-drive vehicle thundered up the bed of the famed **Canyon de Chelly** near **Chinle.**

The brilliant greens against a backdrop of the salmon-color towering cliffs blended with the pink sand of the canyon floor into an eye-dazzling colorama.

Included in the national monument's 131 square miles are the spectacular **Canyon de Chelly** and **Canyon del Muerto**—and many ruins of long-deserted villages.

Johnny Guerro, the Navajo driver-guide, skillfully pushed the truck with its load of eager sightseers into the awesome canyon that once sheltered prehistoric Pueblo Indians.

Today some 100 Navajos call the canyons their summer home, tending their flocks, gardens and orchards. Their hogans, modernized with tar paper roofs and windows, peach orchards and corn crops add to the enchanting atmosphere.

Passengers boarded the open air trucks for a half-day tour of both **Canyon de Chelly** and **Canyon del Muerto** at Justin's Thunderbird Lodge. Hats for protection against the sun were a must.

Johnny, who knows canyon trails and sights from years of experience and ownership of a chunk of canyon land, delighted his guests with descriptions and running patter.

"Afternoon trips in the heat," he quipped, "are called the shake and bake."

The ride was bumpy and jostling as the heavy truck plied through sands of the canyon. Before long, though, passengers learned to "roll with the punches."

"We used smoke signals," continued Johnny, "until the people complained about pollution. Now our trucks have radio communication."

The canyons are full of surprises. There is an abundance of pictographs and petroglyphs, and hundreds of ruins—most built between 350 and 1300 A.D.

Many ruins hang like pictures, perched on ledges or in alcoves along the canyon walls.

At **Antelope House,** built on a stream bank in **Canyon del Muerto,** passengers alighted for a closeup look at the ruins. Shutterbugs had a field day, too, at the **White House Ruins,** named after a long wall in the upper part that is covered with white plaster.

Quicksand, deep dry sand and flash floods make the canyon hazardous. For safety of spectators, protection of fragile ruins and respect for the privacy of the Navajos, visitors are allowed to travel in the canyons only when accompanied by a park ranger or authorized guide. Persons can drive their own 4-wheel drive vehicle in the canyons with a guide.

The one exception, a park spokesman said, is a self-guided mile-long trail from the canyon rim down to the **White House Ruin.** However, half day and all day 4-wheel drive vehicle tours are available for a fee at nearby Justin's Thunderbird Lodge.

"This is a natural scenic area with canyons, cliffs, loose rock and other natural hazards," say rangers. "Make your visit a safe one."

Visitors who do not wish to see the national monument from the ground up, may drive along an area of the south rim of **Canyon de Chelly.** It provides access to five scenic overlooks with warnings of the sheer drops, one at 1,000 feet.

The most spectacular is "Spider Rock." In the late afternoon sun, that spire of sandstone rising 800 feet from the canyon floor at the junction of **Canyon de Chelly** and **Monument Canyon** is a never-to-be forgotten sight.

There are good overnight accommodations in **Chinle** and at Thunderbird Lodge, the latter where a cafeteria offers tasty food at reasonable prices. There are also campground facilities nearby.

Canyon guide explains sights.

White House Ruins are scenic attraction.

Spectacular Spider Rock rises from canyon floor.

SALT RIVER CANYON
salt banks, salt caverns, saltcicles

A fine spray mist was visible over **Apache Falls,** and the **Salt River** shimmered in the sunshine as it coursed through the canyon.

The relatively little known falls are about a half mile upstream from the bridge that spans the **Salt River** on busy **U.S. 60** between **Globe** and **Show Low.**

Visitors can get a close look of the falls by walking over broad, shiny brown rocks that sometimes contain little catch basins of water.

Travelers zipping along the highway admire the canyon from afar, but actually know little about it. The river in that area divides the **Fort Apache Indian Reservation** and the **San Carlos Indian Reservation.** Towering cliffs flank the canyon along the river's meandering course.

Motorists driving off the highway north of the bridge will find a road that forks to the left and leads to the falls. Those who want a longer, more rugged venture can take the fork to the right that heads across **Cibicue Creek** to the **Salt Banks.**

A sign designates the road as primitive. It does curl around mountain areas, but is passable without four-wheel drive for about seven miles to near the **Salt Banks.**

Salt cedars, century plants, mesquite trees, greasewood, varieties of cactus and, surprisingly, yellow and blue flowers dot the area in the late Indian summer.

Four miles down the road, vehicles slosh through **Cibicue Creek** without problem. It's a good idea to determine whether the river is passable before starting to cross. The entire road should be avoided during rainy weather or when there is flooding.

Phil R. Stago, Jr., executive director of the White Mountain Recreation Enterprise on the **Fort Apache Indian Reservation,** says visitors should check with his office in **Whiteriver** to find out if the primitive road and river are passable. There are also a smaller creek and dips in the road.

About three miles farther, a sign marks a turnoff to a picnic area along the **Salt Banks.** The very rough road is not for low-sitting cars.

A trail leads to salt caverns. Stago says "saltcicles" that formed at the top of the caverns sometimes reach the floor. Traditional Indians use the salt for table salt and for ceremonial feasts.

The place is filled with tradition and legends. Stago tells of an area beyond the caverns known as **Chime Rocks,** where boulders have different sounds.

Indians respect the area because it was a place where ceremonials

Salt Cavern area along Salt River

were held.

"It is a place today where Indians go for ceremonial paraphernalia such as yellow clay for the Sunrise Ceremony," Stago says.

The area, however, has been vandalized by persons who do not know or care about its religious significance to the Indians. "We do our best to patrol the area to keep down vandalism," Stago says.

Areas of the canyon also contain nesting grounds for eagles.

"The eagle is a sacred bird to many tribes throughout the country," Stago explains. "We really protect them, especially during the nesting season and when the eagles have their young."

Hunters, fishermen and campers must obtain reservation permits. **Fort Apache** permits can be obtained at the store near the bridge crossing the **Salt River.** The two tribes have agreed to recognize either fishing permit, Stago said.

There are campgrounds along the way with ramadas, tables and restrooms, but no other facilities.

The road continues meandering in the area of the river. "It is definitely advisable to have four-wheel drive vehicles to travel the rest of the road," Stago advised.

WOODRUFF
and damming of the Little Colorado

Lombardy poplars and a patchwork of gardens and old homes near **Blue Butte** blend into a quiet oasis at **Woodruff.**

Uninformed motorists plying the road between **Holbrook** and **Snowflake** would little suspect that a village founded in 1870 lies in the barren hills to the east.

Visitors who veer from **Highway 77** at a sign eight miles south of **Holbrook** and travel a scant five miles on paved highway find the quaintness refreshing.

In a pastoral setting, a little boy with stick in hand shepherds calves down the shaded road.

The Mormon church, heart of the community, stands in quiet dignity, and a tiny post office boasts the U.S. flag and a cluster of pink hollyhocks. Vegetable gardens stretch from houses. A welcome peace pervades.

The community boasts about 50 families, a school for kindergartners and students through the second grade (others are bussed to **Holbrook**), the post office and church.

Woodruff seems little affected by the hurly-burly, fast pace of the late twentieth century. Electricity, street lights, television and the historic water company, however, provide modernization.

Showpiece in the town in a 1972 visit was a fence made of petrified wood at the Earl Crofford home.

Nathan Tenney, a Mormon who came from Brigham City, is considered the founding father. Although there had been others before him, Nathan and his sons were with him when he made permanent camp and called the settlement "Tenney's Camp" in 1877. A year later the name was changed to **Woodruff** in honor of Wilford Woodruff, a Mormon church president.

Others came to settle in the Indian Territory, and for a time they lived in the protection of a fort. After the danger of hostile Indians was over, the first families began building outside the fort. Historians note that the land on which the town was built was owned by the Atlantic and Pacific Railroad Co. In February, 1882, the townsite was surveyed and purchased from the railroad company for $8 per acre.

The story of **Woodruff,** some say, is its relentless quest for a source of irrigation water for crops and the damming of the **Little Colorado River.** The soil was fertile and the supply of water in the river ample. But, 13 dams washed away before the 14th and successful one was built in 1918 at the confluence of **Silver Creek,** and the **Little**

Colorado, three miles from **Woodruff.**

Old timers can talk about the time **Lyman Dam** near **St. Johns** cracked and a wall of water flooded the 13th dam. The first rush of muddy water overflowed ditches and ran into the streets. In a thunderous roar, the dam broke and the water rushed down the stream.

Woodruff became known as the "Garden Spot of the West," and people from miles around came to enjoy its produce. Today, many who live here work in **Holbrook.**

Blue Butte, towering 5,616 ft., was once the scene of Indian ceremonies. Medicine men of old sang out in the night heralding ceremonies.

A rock "fence" on the butte is visible in places. Oldsters here say it was built to keep the Hash Knife Cattle from coming into town and eating the crops.

A round trip to **Woodruff** from **Phoenix** can be made in a day, but the outing is more leisurely with stops in **Payson,** an overnight stay in **Holbrook** and a return trip on **Highway 99** out of **Winslow.**

Famous fence of petrified wood at Woodruff

CONCHO
just a shell of its former self!

Old rock and adobe houses, weathered and abandoned, lend a ghost town air to this crossroads hamlet in Apache County.

Concho, from a Greek work meaning shell, lives up to its name. The village, nestling in a saucer-like valley 30 miles northeast of **Show Low** at the junction of **Arizona 180** and **61,** is a mere shell of its once-thriving self.

The reddish-brown adobe and rock houses contrast interestingly with lombardy poplars and spreading cottonwood trees. Some crumbling buildings are topless. Occasionally a lone wall remains, its yesteryear doorway gaping with a picture view of the valley.

The forlorn houses have a certain fascination for the viewer. Near one vacant house, with two stories and high-peaked roof, a roadside table and benches invited a picnic or quiet rest.

Among livable houses, one boasted a sweeping veranda, another curtained windows. **Concho** in 1968 also included the San Rafael Catholic Church, a small school, trading post, bar, store, post office and population of 125.

Pastoral charm and quiet spelled **Concho's** appeal to visitors. Piglets scampered on a dirt road at the approach of a car. A sign on a fence marked the office of the justice of the peace and irrigation water sparkled in the sun in a field of corn. Elsewhere, frisky children escorted a milk cow to greener pastures.

Concho was founded in the 1870's by the Candeleria family, who established a sheep-raising enterprise. In 1879, Mormon families moved in from Utah and established a ward near the Spanish settlement. In time, they moved on to **St. Johns.**

Sheep-raising flourished for decades, but, according to one resident, cattlemen bought up much of the land, putting an end to much of the free grazing. There were other factors that helped spell **Concho's** decline. Younger generations of the sheep families did not want to live in sheep camps, preferring instead a more modern life. World War II siphoned off many young men, who afterward did not return. Older generations moved on to join their children.

In **Concho's** regression, old adobe houses were left behind. Agriculture is a principal occupation. Spring water feeds nearby **Concho Lake,** which was dammed for water to irrigate the crops. The dam is described as the oldest ever constructed by whites in Arizona for irrigation purposes.

In 1922, **Concho** was reported as the richest little town in northern Arizona. There was a bank, three or four stores, and a population of 300.

Doorway of old house opens to picture view of Concho.

Styled in old adobe

119

Fort Apache Indian Reservation

A swing through the **Fort Apache Indian Reservation** in north-central Arizona offers eye-feasting scenery and an insight into its people and culture.

The reservation covers 1,664,372 acres and is the home of more than 4,000 Apaches. It is said to contain 26 lakes, 300 miles of trout streams, public campsites and big game, all of interest to sportsmen and outdoor fans.

But, even for the casual tourist, the reservation offers interesting variety.

There are trading posts, ancient ruins, an old Apache fort including Gen. George Crook's former home, wickiups, hospitable Apaches and history galore.

Starting point for a two-day venture into Indian land can be **State Highway 73** out of **Carrizo Junction** at **U.S. Highway 60.** In no time, the trek into the juniper and red earth country takes motorists to **Cedar Creek** and just past the John F. Kennedy School.

The Cedar Creek Trading Post, with its array of blankets, hats and beadwork, offers a good place to stop, browse and enjoy a touch of Indian atmosphere.

History buffs will find several sites to please them. **Kinishba Ruins,** reached by a two-mile dirt and gravel road off the paved highway, are more than 1,000 years old and protected by fence.

The ruins are not far from **Ft. Apache,** established in 1870 to control Navajos and Apaches. It was manned by the U.S. Cavalry until 1924 when it was turned over to the Indian Service for use as a school.

The fort was a training camp for Indian scouts and was commanded by several officers of historical importance, including Crook, whose home has been converted into a museum.

The museum contains pictures, legends and artifacts of Indian culture. Museum guide Ann Qyezzie said the building is open 8 a.m. to 5 p.m. weekdays and weekends in summer.

A map of the **Fort Apache Reservation,** available at the museum, notes that some reservation roads are closed to public travel and suggests contacting **Whiteriver** headquarters if in doubt.

Beyond Whiteriver, a side road leads off **State Highway 73** to the **Alchesay Hatchery,** named for a famous Apache chief.

Whiteriver itself, the tribal headquarters, bustles with the activity of trading posts, a hospital, school and office of the White Mountain Apache Enterprise, where Indian bracelets and jewelry are available. On Chief Street, many of the Indian women wear traditional squaw dresses, adding a note of authenticity and color to the Apacheland

Kinishba ruins on Fort Apache Reservation

town.

From another vantage point on the reservation, the wind moaned around a fire lookout tower, high above the forests of the reservation.

Floyd Dosela knew from radio communications that a log was on fire at **Hawley Lake.**

Dosela's wife, Lenda, with their young daughter nearby, occasionally picked up the binoculars and scanned the horizon. In the distance could be seen the McNary Lumber mill and **Hawley Lake.**

Dosela and his family spend the summer on the 9,000-ft. **McKay Peak,** living in a little house near the base of the tower. He climbs the 50-foot structure to keep his 7 a.m. to 7 p.m. vigil seven days a week.

He is one of the many who help the 1.6 million-acre reservation provide a growing recreation center for Arizona.

A reservation brochure explains: "The pride and fierceness, skill and endurance of the Apaches, once used to defend their land from the white man, now helps draw the American public to Apacheland."

A trip to **McKay Peak,** south of **Hawley Lake,** is an endurance test. The last quarter mile of the trail is made on foot, and climbers should be in good condition. The venturesome may visit the lookout point 9 a.m. to 5 p.m.

A scenic treat is in store for motorists veering off **State 260** and on to **State 473** enroute to **Hawley Lake.** The North Fork of **White River** at McCoy Bridge is picture-pretty, and it is not unusual to see fishermen fly-casting for trout. Nearby are campgrounds. Camping and fishing permits are required on the reservation.

The reservation abounds with wildlife. A forest sign warns that "Bears are wild and dangerous animals. Don't feed them. Remain in the vehicle with windows up while observing the bears."

Otherwise, the reservation forests are friendly and among the most beautiful in the state.

WHITE MOUNTAINS
autumn wonderland of color

Mother Nature stages one of her finest shows in the Arizona northlands. Starring in the production are the aspens quaking in their golden costumes.

Perhaps the greatest stanza in the annual autumn song of the forest occurs in the **Alpine** area, along a lap of the famed **Coronado Trail, U.S. 666.**

There, the "quakies" flow around the mountain slopes in gorgeous golds and oranges. In a golden "bowl" about two miles south of **Alpine,** the aspens with their whitebarked trunks are a joy to behold.

"It's mind-boggling," exclaimed a woman who journeyed from **Tucson** to see the fall foliage.

A visitor from Mesa who was aiming his camera, called the show "spectacular."

"I came up here to see the fall colors," he said. "This is more than I imagined."

There are tall aspens, their yellow dressing tipped with red, oak leaves in burnished bronze, sumac in "fire chief" reds, ferns in yellow with brown flecks and, of course, the tall pines and blue-green silver spruce.

Other forest areas are also in elegant foliage. Sixteen miles east of **Pinetop** along **State Highway 260,** the forest was a showplace, as aspen clusters sparkled in brilliance among the evergreens. Occasionally, a lone aspen stood in solitude in regal contrast.

Drawing admiration, too, was **A-1 Lake,** nestled near the highway and mirroring the brilliant yellow aspens.

Our party, satiated with the yellow beauty in the **Pinetop-Greer** area, capped the fun by spending the night at **White Mountain Lodge** in **Greer.** Yellow aspen leaves adorned a blackbear skin on the wall of the lodge's living room.

After a roast beef and apple pie dinner, lodge guests exchanged travel notes and other tales. Breakfasters appreciated the toasty warmth from the fire place.

With **Greer** as the early morning starting point, the distance to the **Coronado Trail** wasn't great. Our itinerary went as far south on **U.S. 666** as **Hannagan Meadow.**

The annual golden show truly is a balm to pressure-jaded city spirits. It's a heyday, too, for camera buffs.

As the song of the forest progresses in its final stanza, the aspen leaves dance in the breeze, then ultimately lose their fragile grip and

flutter to the ground.
  Winter snows can't be too far away.

Yellow-clad aspens bask in autumn sun.

THE CORONADO TRAIL
copper mines to high forest—
a backwoods wonderland!

The **Coronado Trail** and late fall combine for unique travel fare.
During a tour in late November, most riotously-colored leaves had fallen, except on the lower end of the trail. There, yellow foliage clung to cottonwoods and fragmented leaves clutched like red crumbs to maple trees. Even the red sumac lingered in clusters here and there.

The aspens, quaking in white nakedness, were in somber contrast to the blue spruce, ponderosa pine and Douglas fir. Basking in the sun or muted shadows, the forest, as at any time of the year, was in spectacular beauty.

The **Coronado Trail,** named for Spanish explorer Francisco Vasquez de Coronado who came through the area in 1540, offers rugged beauty for modern day travelers.

The trail's scenery has long been famous, and a few Arizonans remember when it was a one-car trail. The highway, now fully paved, is virtually free of signboards save the welcome markers by the U.S. Forest Service. Gas and groceries are not available from **Clifton** to **Hannagan Meadow.**

The trail may be prefaced with a stop at the huge open copper pit at **Morenci.**

From the Coronado Trail's starting point **State Route 666** north of **Highway 70,** south of **Clifton** to its end at **Springerville,** the drive, towering at 9,200 feet, twisting and dipping with steep drops in some areas, is a fast-changing scenic bonanza.

Openers for the trail is the stretch along the **Morenci** mining area, flanked by a towering man-made mountain of mine waste rock and rugged natural mountains. The area to **Metcalf** is pock-marked by mines and tunnels, all to be avoided.

It was at **Metcalf,** now a crumbling ghost town, where the first productive copper mines in Arizona reportedly began. One story tells that cavalrymen Bob and Jim Metcalf were in pursuit of Indians in 1870 in the area and had camped at **Clifton.** Bob located rich deposits of copper and later staked claims.

The Shannon Copper Co. began producing copper there in 1901, and the community became known as **Metcalf.** By 1910, nearly 5,000 people lived there.

Another story notes that the first railroads in Arizona were two lines competing to haul copper ore from **Metcalf** to **Morenci.** Today two sets of tunnels mark their trail.

Twin tunnels mark early rail competition.

At Hannagan Meadow

Part of **Metcalf** is buried by mine slag, including the old cemetery where bodies were first removed. A marker along the road proclaims the old town of **Metcalf** and another lists the miners who died there. An old bank vault stands forlornly along the way and stairs to another building obviously lead nowhere now.

The **Coronado Trail** picks up new tones as the red-beige rocks of the mining area give way to sparse vegetation, then coils through scrub oaks, sycamores and cottonwoods. In higher elevations the deciduous trees were minus their dress of leaves.

A side trip to **Eagle Creek** on a turnoff about 25 miles north of **Clifton** offered another change of pace.

Meandering along
"THE BLUE"

One minute, we were parking our car by a time-weathered stone building, once the post office for this corner of forest tranquility.

Minutes later we were splashing through the nearby **Blue River.** Bold signs near the bank said "Slow" and "Ford."

Ford we did—after advice of a localite and a sizeup of the river flow. The Jeep headed through the shallow tan waters without a whimper and nosed ahead toward a double-trailer home nearby. A roadside marker heralded **"Joyville."**

J. E. "Slim" Joy, who first came here in 1926, knows the country and its people. In time, he owned a share of the scenic remoteness. Actually, there is no town of Blue per se. Most folks today refer to **"The Blue"** as that strip where sprawling ranches nestle in varied proximity of the meandering river.

Our trip to **Blue** had been in the mill for months, and everytime we mentioned **Blue,** the most often response was, "Where's that? I never heard of it."

That only heightened the desire to visit the place.

The Blue is reached by turning on a gravel road near the Luna Bar on **U.S. 180,** just east of **Alpine.** The mountain village of **Alpine** is along the famed **Coronado Trail, U.S. 666,** and some 25 miles south of **Springerville.** At times the gravel road to **The Blue Country** snakes inside and out of New Mexico. Actually, the old post office (it was relocated), in the heart of the better-known **Blue** area, is 22 miles from the gravel road turnoff.

An Apache-Sitgreaves National Forest map is available at the Alpine Ranger Station, and, actually, a night in **Alpine** provides the advantage of an early start to Blue.

The road corkscrews downward, hugging canyon walls and requiring caution from start to finish—specially after a rain. The trip should be avoided in times of rain because of water runoffs, swollen washes and the river that can rampage. Elevation drops from **Alpine's** 8,046 feet to some 6,000 feet.

The hideaway beauty is ethereal—pines, walnut, aspen cedar, boxelders, sycamores, entwining vines—quaint one-way bridges towering beige rock cliffs—the rippling Blue which heads in the New Mexico mountains.

Chipmunks, rabbits and squirrels dart across the road and, in the summer, purple thistle, white poppies, Indian paint brush flowers in brilliant red and blackeyed Susans, are beauty notes.

It was a travel sashay to be remembered.

Fording The Blue

Old rock building with idle pump—former post office

One-way bridge through "The Blue" country

The Blue School House, in white and red and fronted with a huge alligator juniper, had three students last year.

Mrs. Tom Cielak, wife of the teacher, was busy with Saturday affairs while her child watched television. Two large shepherd dogs ambled about.

"I really enjoy living here," said Mrs. Cielak of life in the remote area. "The community is real neat. I've never seen any place where people are so close."

Bears have been seen, and there was the time when javelinas chased her dogs. The dogs keep wild animals away, she said, or at least alert the family when they venture close.

About 50 people, give or take a few, live along The Blue, including those on sprawling ranches. On a summer Saturday only two sets of picknickers were at the **Blue Crossing** and **Upper Blue Campgrounds.** Motorists should bring along food and ample gasoline for the return trip. The old gasoline pump by the rock building is idle.

(Unexpected notes on the July, 1981, trip were the "plague" signs, posted by the Greenlee County Health Department. An Arizona State Health Dept. official, speaking on the bubonic plague, said that months ago an infected field mouse had been found. Signs list basic precautions. A new surveillance check was planned, he said.)

At **"Joyville,"** just across the **Blue,** Joy was working in his vegetable garden, his two dogs meandering about. Joy served as postmaster here 26 years, and his wife, Marjorie, succeeded him. She retired three years ago. The couple once operated a hunting lodge here.

"When I first came to this country, it was paradise," he said. "It is one of the best places I know to live now. You are out of the rat race. I love the mountain air."

Mail is delivered here from Alpine three times a week in the summer and twice a week in the winter. A post office was established in the area in 1898 under the name of **Whittum.** Four years later it was changed to **Blue,** because the name was more identifying.

Arizona Republic files note the post office in 1963 was probably the most remote in Arizona. It made Ripley's "Believe It or Not" as the furthermost from a trans-continental railroad, there being 141 miles to the Santa Fe in **Holbrook** and 153 miles to the Southern Pacific in **Lordsburg.** Once **Blue** was cut off from **Alpine** 13 days because of snow.

A doctor and his wife, also an MD, live in the area. The school house now contains a library, operated by the Blue River Cowbelles, wives of cattlemen.

Besides television, the Joy home boasts a dial telephone.

"I was here before they had anything but a whoop-and-holler telephone," Joy said, chuckling.

The couple enjoys the tranquility and the people of The Blue.

"It's just like one big family," said Mrs. Joy.

The Blue School is remote seat of learning.

SOUTHEAST ARIZONA

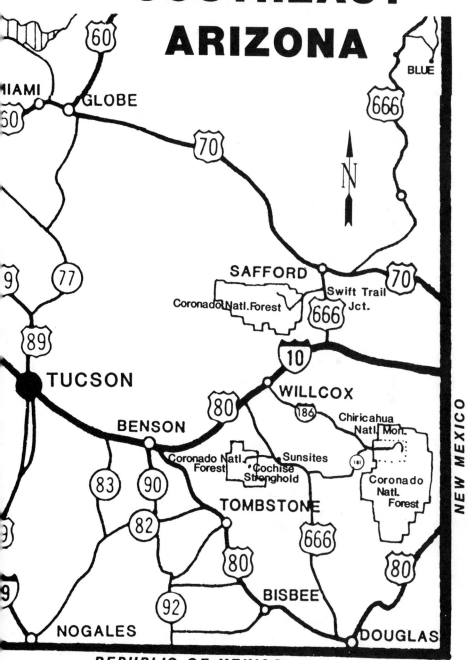

THE SWIFT TRAIL
autumn-time
in Graham Mountains

Autumn is painting the high recesses of the **Pinaleno Mountains** into a forest fantasy land.

Even in late September, after lingering warmth and before the full fall rash of color, the trail offered changing panoramas.

There were touches of gold in the quaking aspen leaves and daisies that clustered in roadside bouquets. In spiraling heights, ferns that once carpeted the forest in green were of bronze hue.

The trail out of **Safford** should be traveled leisurely to fully savor the fall stanza that hovers all too fragilely for a short span.

In a forest vine leaf, the green was changing to gold and brilliant red, artfully threaded with delicate veins. And, hanging from a bush beneath a tall tree, was a cluster of berries in shiny maroon red. Not knowing the variety, viewers left the berries unsampled.

In higher altitudes, the golds meshed with the green of spruce and ponderosa pine, Douglas fir and corkbark firs. Little acorns were maturing on scrub oaks and, overall, a spicy aroma pervaded the forest.

The trail is named in honor of Theodore T. Swift, supervisor of **Crook National Forest** from 1910 to 1923.

Vegetation varies with elevation. At the start, there are mesquite and creosote bush. In the low foothills are prickly pear, ocotillo and sotol. Forest trees star in higher altitudes. At **Heliograph Peak** the elevation is 10,028 feet.

Wet canyon picnic grounds were noisy with the rush of a mountain stream, and vining red leaves entwined old trees. Traveling on, every turn in the trail revealed eye-catching vistas of the forest.

Arcadia Campground, at elevation 6,700 feet, requires a small fee, as do most picnic and camp areas.

At **Lady Bug Saddle,** elevation 8,500 feet, the trail crosses over the south side of **Graham Mountains.** The name is derived from the large number of ladybugs concentrated here at certain seasons.

Our party chose to take Side Trip No. 1 to Forest Service Lookout Tower on **Heliograph Peak.** The road was rough—but what a view!

The peak is so named because it was used in early days as an Army heliograph station. Signals were given by means of a mirror and sunlight, enabling the Army to communicate from station to station in southern Arizona. The 100-foot steel tower is manned during the critical fire season, normally May 1 to July 31.

Heliograph fire lookout tower

Back on the trail, there are side roads to **Shannon Campground, Graham Peak** and **Treasure Park,** where, according to a report, 19 pack loads of stolen gold and silver were buried by Mexican bandits before the Gadsen Purchase. We did not check out this believe-it-or-not tale.

At **Riggs Flat Lake,** elevation 8,600 feet, picnicking in the quiet forest scene was well worth the fee. The dam for this 11-acre lake was financed in 1957 by the Arizona Game and Fish Department to provide public trout fishing.

A round trip out of **Safford** to the crest of **Mount Graham,** exclusive of side trips, is 84 miles. Total driving time (again exclusive of side trips) is four and a half hours. There are no service stations on the **Swift Trail,** a two-lane paved road for 22 miles. It then becomes a curving, graveled road.

Precautions: Watch for signs displayed during logging truck activity, drive carefully, and stay on the right side of the road.

Some camping areas close normally at the end of September, or they may remain open longer, depending on the weather. The trail will remain open until after the snow falls.

A free brochure for the **Swift Trail,** detailing mileage and many facets, including an apple orchard, is available from the Ranger Station, located in **Safford** in the post office building. The office is open from 8 a.m. to 5 p.m., except noon. The brochure, also, may be obtained by mail. The return trip on the **Swift Trail** is via the same road. To get an early start on the trail, we spent the night at a motel in **Safford.**

A perfect finale occurred along the way on our return trip. A fawn stood beside the road, then bounced up the mountainside at the car's approach.

The timid forest creature then stared at us from behind a bush. Its delicate, inquisitive face was a sight to behold. And remember.

CHIRICAHUA NATIONAL MONUMENT
Arizona's Wonderland of Rocks

Giant formations mesh in grandeur and fantasy to create a sur-realistic, other-world effect in the **Wonderland of Rocks.**

Colossal boulders in the **"Heart of the Rocks"** area loom in fanciful likeness of people and animals. Balanced rocks, spires, pinnacles and great pillared cliffs add vistas of splendor in these rugged mountains, 36 miles southwest of **Willcox.**

The scenic prize, however, is not achieved without strenuous effort, as a party of hikers from the **Valley of the Sun** discovered on this remote trek.

"Any way you look at it," the genial ranger at the park station told them, "the complete hike to the **Heart of the Rocks** is eight miles, but if you start from **Massai Point,** much of the hike will be down hill. We'll shuttle you back to pick up your car."

Heart of the Rocks, locale of major named rock formations, provides the most rugged and rewarding hiking, along a one-mile loop skirting canyons of rocks.

Geologists believe that millions of years ago the **Chiricahua** region, then a level plain, was shaken by a series of violent and explosive volcanic eruptions.

Glowing clouds of gas, carrying tremendous quantities of white-hot ash and volcanic sand, spread rapidly from the mouth of the volcano. As each cloud cooled, the solid particles were bonded together to form great thicknesses of solid rock.

Erosion still goes on, slowly and persistently. Pedestal or balanced rocks have formed and fallen; others are tottering; more are just taking shape. Within a human lifetime, only minor changes may be noticed, but with the passage of centuries the face of the land shows vast changes.

A trail stems from **Massai Point** (altitude 6,870 ft.). On this partic-ular day, hikers clad in warm clothing and sturdy walking shoes left at 10:20 a.m. in windy cold. It was 4:03 p.m. before they emerged—complete with aching muscles.

The aches disappeared, but the scenic beauty was unforgettable. The path, sometimes carpeted with pine needles and even snow, wound past cypress trees, manzanita, pines and alligator junipers. Lizards dashed up boulders and birds chirped at the intrusion.

Cottontails, kangaroo rats, skunks, foxes, coyotes and raccoons inhabit the park. The Valley hiking party encountered a curious coati-

Curious coati at Chiricahua

Camel's head

Mushroom rock

mundi at the picnic ground.

Many rest stops were made during the rugged-climb areas. A pause at the summit revealed a panoramic view of **Cochise Head Mountain** and a reminder that Apache Indians once roamed the area.

After the **Heart of the Rocks** loop, there remained 3½ miles mostly in descent. Hikers coped with gravel that skidded beneath the feet. A sign in the park, "watch out for falling rocks," suggested another hazard.

Visitors are required to stop at the Visitor Center to pay a park entrance fee.

LAND OF COCHISE
Coronado National Forest and Wonderland of Rocks

Arizonans with a yen to vacation in Arizona may want to sample travel treats in Cochise County.

On a four-day trek in the southeastern Arizona Country visiting places of fantastic scenery, we had a ball. It was, however, the first time I ever backed 10 miles into **Tombstone.** More of that later.

Cochise County travel tempts those who like to mix adventure with their vacation.

There are pure scenic attractions in the vastness of the **Coronado National Forest,** an historic outlaw's final resting place, a famed Indian chieftain's stronghold, plus a roster of ghost towns still wreathed in the aura of the Old West.

Some scenic attractions can be enjoyed in the summer as they are in the cool recesses of towering mountains.

Taking the cake, in our opinion, from the standpoint of pure beauty, is **Rustler Park.** It is reached out of **Willcox** on **State 186,** verging on **181,** about 2.5 miles to the turnoff to **Rustler Park** area, and then a climb into the mountains.

The sylvan beauty in **Rustler Park,** so named because it was a haven for rustlers in the 1870's, is breathtaking. Consider ferns, sumac, pines, oak, wild grapevines, wild yellow flowers, an 8,754 ft. altitude and even a murmuring brook stemming from a spring.

A rustic corral stirred speculation about the long-ago rustlers. There was a ranger station, picnic facilities, water, restrooms and only two other families during our visit. The descent offered panoramic views of the valley below.

On another sashay along **Turkey Creek Road,** our party was delighted to find the grave of the famed (or infamous) Arizona outlaw, Johnny Ringo. A plaque installed by the Cochise County Archaeological and Historical Society and the Arizona Historical Society reads:

"The remains of the noted gunman and outlaw lie here. A teamster traveling from West Turkey Creek found the outlaw sitting in the fork of a nearby oak tree with a bullet hole in the right temple. A coroner's jury reported the death to be a suicide and Ringo was buried on the spot. There were others who viewed the body and maintained that the July 13, 1882, death of Ringo was murder."

The stone mounded grave is alongside **Turkey Creek Road,** about 4.5 miles off **State 181,** and takes close observation to find. The crude

Bathtub Lake in Rucker Canyon area

carved stone marker lying beside the forked oak provides a thoughtful interlude for history buffs.

History fans also will appreciate the many ghost towns—**Gleeson, Pearce, Courtland, Charleston, Dos Cabezas** (still lively), the old **Fort Bowie** and the far-from-ghostly **Tombstone.**

A scenic attraction bound to delight is the **Wonderland of Rocks** in the **Chiricahua National Monument,** some 49 miles south of **Willcox.**

Most national park areas offer camping and picnic sites.

A case in point and probably less known is **Cochise Stronghold,** the home and refuge of the crafty Indian chief, Cochise, and his Chiricahua Apache followers so long ago. They could sweep down the natural stone fortress, attack and return to safety.

The area is reached by turning off **Interstate 10** about nine miles southwest of **Willcox** onto **U.S. 666.** A turn on a gravel road near **Sunsites,** and a 10-mile drive will put visitors into the stronghold in the **Coronado National Forest.**

On our visit, we paid a $2 national forest fee to picnic there. The cooing doves, a gentle breeze, the shade, the colorful surroundings blended pleasingly even on a hot July day. A marked nature trail provided exercise and a chance to learn about native flora.

A vacationer there identified finches, doves, jays, lizards, snakes (including rattlers), badgers, manzanita, alligator juniper and Arizona cypress trees among others.

Ranger station in cool Rustler Park

Johnny Ringo's marker along Turkey Creek

Rucker Canyon Recreation Area, in another part of the **Coronado National Forest,** also is rewarding. **"Bathtub" Lake** was picturesque. **Camp Rucker,** an important military post in the Indian campaign, was in the area. The camp is said to be named for a young military officer who gave his life trying to save a fellow officer during a flash flood.

Picnicking at the site (here again we paid the $2 fee) was pleasant in the cool altitude of about 6,500 feet.

It must be remembered most mountain scenic places are reached by gravel roads, some rain-ravaged with washes, and sometimes narrow and rough. Gasoline, food and water should accompany travelers, and, don't forget *maps.*

Our party was dismayed at **Rustler Park** to find the car battery had come loose and rested on the manifold. One cell was dead. We managed to get 10 miles from **Tombstone** before the battery conked out completely. Two Mountain Bell employees, after trying to help, radioed in for a wrecker.

The wrecker arrived in 30 minutes, but it was the first time I ever rode backwards in a car. All this did not diminish our enthusiasm. Our reservations were secure at the Lookout Lodge in **Tombstone.**

There are so many places of interest in Cochise County that to visit them is certainly not a one-day stand. We spent a night each in **Willcox, Douglas,** and **Tombstone.** It's a good idea to have motel reservations.

The Cochise Visitor Center and Museum at **Willcox** offers free brochures and information about what to see and when.

INDEX of PLACE NAMES

Dates in parentheses identify the author's most recent visit.

ORDER BLANK

MasterCard Golden West Publishers VISA

4113 N. Longview Ave. • Phoenix, AZ 85014

Please ship the following books: 602-265-4392

Number of Copies		Per Copy	AMOUNT
	Arizona Adventure	5.95	
	Arizona—Off the Beaten Path	5.95	
	Arizona Legends and Lore	5.95	
	Arizona Outdoor Guide	5.95	
	Bill Williams Mountain Men	5.00	
	Conflict at the Border	5.00	
	Cowboy Slang	5.95	
	Destination: Grand Canyon	5.00	
	Discover Arizona	5.00	
	Explore Arizona	5.00	
	Ghost Towns in Arizona	5.95	
	Hiking Arizona	5.95	
	In Old Arizona	5.95	
	Mavericks	5.00	
	Old West Adventures in Arizona	5.95	
	On the Arizona Road	5.00	
	Prehistoric Arizona	5.00	
	Quest for the Dutchman's Gold	6.95	
	Southwest Saga	5.95	
	Verde River Recreation Guide	5.95	
	Wild West Characters	5.95	
Add $1.50 to total order for shipping & handling			$1.50

☐ My Check or Money Order Enclosed . . . . $ _____

☐ MasterCard   ☐ VISA

Acct. No. _____ Exp. Date _____

Signature _____

Name _____

Address _____

City/State/Zip _____

This order blank may be photo-copied.

AZ Path

MasterCard and VISA Orders Accepted ($20 Minimum)

Books from Golden West Publishers

Ghost Towns and Historic Haunts in Arizona—
Visit the silver cities of Arizona's golden past with
this prize-winning reporter-photographer. Come
along to the towns whose heydays were once wild
and wicked! Crumbling adobe walls, old mines,
cemeteries, cabins and castles. (144 pages) ... **$5.95**

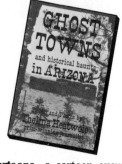

Cowboy Country Cartoons—a cartoon excursion through the whimsical west of renowned
cowboy cartoonist-sculptor Jim Willoughby. West
humor at its ribald best! 128 pages) ...**$4.50**

Southwestern frontier tales more thrilling than
fiction. Trimble brings history to life with humor, pathos and irony of pioneer lives: territorial
politics, bungled burglaries, shady deals, frontier
lawmen, fighting editors, Baron of Arizona,
horse and buggy doctors, etc. *In Old Arizona*
by Marshall Trimble (160 pages) ...*$5.95*

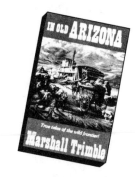

Southwest Saga—the way it really was, by
Southwest historian-journalist William C.
McGaw—Esteban's life among the Zuni, Pancho
Villa's raid north of the border, Mark Twain's
drug scheme, the strange death of Ambrose
Bierce, etc. (160 pages) ...*$5.95*

Ride the back trails with modern-day mountain
men, as they preserve the memory of Arizona's
rugged adventurers of the past. Buckskin-clad,
the mountain men stage annual treks from
Williams, AZ all the way to Phoenix, AZ and
to other destinations. Hiliarious anecdotes of
hard-riding men. *Bill Williams Mountain Men*
by Thomas E. Way (128 pages) ...*$5.00*

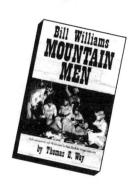